CASTLES
FROM THE
HEART OF SPAIN

ALBERTO A. WEISSMÜLLER

photographs
by the author

 *Clarkson N. Potter, Inc./Publisher* NEW YORK

Published by Clarkson N. Potter Inc. New York.
Library of Congress Catalog Card No. 67/24607.
Text set by Harrison & Sons (Westminster) Limited, 20/22 Bedfordbury,
London, W.C.2.
Printed by Compton Printing Limited, Pembroke Road, Stocklake,
Aylesbury, Bucks.
Jackets and colour section printed by Weather Oak Press Limited,
Graphic House, Lower Essex Street, Birmingham 5.

© Design Year Book Limited 1967. in Great Britain
Art Director: Ian Cameron.
House Editor: Elizabeth Kingsley-Rowe.
Designer: Jacque Solomons.
First Published 1967.
Printed in England.
Plans and Maps drawn by G Wall with the exception of Château
Gaillard (Page 34) by Sidney Toy .F.S.A. F.R.I.B.A. by kind per-
mission of Alaric Toy.

To Constance, who made this book possible

CONTENTS

Page

LIST OF ILLUSTRATIONS 9
PREFACE 11
INTRODUCTION 13
SPAIN AND ISLAM 14
SPAIN AND EUROPE 32
BASIC STAGES OF SPANISH CASTLE
  BUILDING 40
THE PROVINCE OF VALLADOLID .. 56
Peñafiel 58
La Mota, Medina del Campo 67
Fuensaldaña 75
Simancas 80

THE PROVINCES OF SORIA,
  GUADALAJARA AND CUENCA .. 84
Osma 86
Gormaz 88
Atienza 91
Sigüenza 94
Torija 96
Haro 99
Belmonte 99

THE PROVINCE OF AVILA 106
The City of Avila .. .. .: .. 106
Villaviciosa 111
Mombeltrán 113
Arenas de San Pedro 117
Arévalo 119
Las Navas del Marqués 123

THE PROVINCE OF SEGOVIA 124
Turégano 126
Coca 128
Pedraza 133
Cuéllar 137

Castilnovo 140
Alcázar of Segovia 142

THE PROVINCE OF MADRID 146
Alcázar of Madrid 149
Buitrago 150
El Real de Manzanares 154
San Martín de Valdeiglesias 159
Villarejo de Salvanes 161
Chinchón 162
Alcalá de Henares 163
Villaviciosa de Odón 164

THE PROVINCE OF TOLEDO 166
The Bridges of Alcántara & San Martín .. 168
San Servando 171
Las Guadalerzas 173
Barciense 173
Escalona 175
Guadamur 183
Alcázar of Toledo 186

SPANISH MILITARY ORDERS 190
Calatrava la Vieja 209
Calatrava la Nueva 210
Zorita de los Canes 212
Anguix 217
Maqueda 218
Consuegra 221

LIST OF ILLUSTRATIONS

Alcalá de Guadaira 45, 130
Alcalá de Henares 163
Alcázar of Segovia 2, 46, 77, 125, 143, 144, 145, 191
Alcázar of Toledo 167, 189
Anguix 155
Arenas de San Pedro 117, 118
Arévalo 119, 120
Atienza 92, 93, 182
Avila 54, 107, 108, 109, 110
Barciense 174, 175
Belmonte 36, 100, 101, 102, 104. 105
Bridge of Alcántara 169
Bridge of San Martín 168
Buitrago 151, 152, 153
Calatrava La Nueva 19, 195, 197, 198, 199, 206, 211
Calatrava La Vieja 192, 193, 196, 200, 208, 209, 212,
   215
Carmona 30, 31
Castilnovo 140, 141, 142
Chinchón 162
Coca 129
Consuegra 221, 222
Cuéllar 137, 138, 139
Escalona 43, 176, 177, 179, 180, 181, 183
Fuensaldaña 76, 79, 81
Gibralfaro 35
Gormaz 90, 207
Las Guadalerzas 173
Guadamur 184, 185
Haro 78
Maqueda 202, 203, 220
Mombeltrán 38, 44, 113, 114, 115, 116
Montealegre 16, 21, 23
La Mota, Medina del Campo 33, 66, 67, 68, 69, 70,
   71, 72, 73, 74, 75
Las Navas del Marqués (Magalia) 121, 122, 123
Osma 86
Pedraza 37, 49, 82, 132, 133, 134, 135, 136
Peñafiel 17, 25, 49, 50, 51, 57, 58, 59, 62, 63, 64, 65
El Real de Manzanares 147, 156, 158
San Martín de Valdeiglesias 47, 159, 160
San Servando 170
Sigüenza 103
Simancas 83
Tordesillas 22
Torija 41, 97, 98
Torrelobatón 26, 28, 42, 48, 50, 52, 53
Turégano 27
Villarejo de Salvanes 161
Villaviciosa (Avila) 55, 112
Villaviciosa de Odón 165
Zorita de los Canes 201, 204, 208, 213, 214, 219

PREFACE

The author is indebted to a number of people and institutions for advice and source material in preparing this book. The late Sidney Toy, FSA, FRIBA, London, with his encouragement in the early stages, was among them, and it is hoped that the final result would have met his stern requirements. Thanks to his son and literary executor, Alaric Toy, a plan of Château Gaillard has been included.

Particularly useful to me was the most generous advice provided by Don Angel Dotor Municio, the erudite Director of the Asociación Española de Amigos de los Castillos, Madrid; as well as the kind help received from the Count of Gamazo, Madrid, and from Dr. John Halstead of the New York State University at Buffalo, New York.

I am also indebted to Miss Olga Raggio, Associate Curator of Western European Arts at the Metropolitan Museum of Art, New York, for her help in the preparation of the Introduction and the material for the castle of El Real de Manzanares.

Finally, the author must acknowledge and thank the Hispanic Institute of New York for making available, through the kind co-operation of Mrs. B. Graham Proske, its photographic archives and library.

The author would like to convey to all those who have helped and encouraged him in his task his sincere thanks and appreciation, and would like to think that their time and efforts have not been spent in vain.

Needless to say, although many sources have been used, as indicated below, the opinions expressed in the book are those of the author.

Anyone interested in Spanish castles has an advantage if he can read Spanish, since there is a great and valuable body of material on them which has not been translated. Many Spaniards are not indifferent to their magnificent castles and a serious effort to study and restore them is presently being made. Perhaps no organisation has done so more to increase the popular feeling for castles than the Asociación Española de Amigos de los Castillos, whose President at this time is the Marquis de Sales. The Asociación has tried to fill the gap, at least in part, in books on Spanish castles translated into other languages. Its effort is the commendable *Castles Itinerary In Castile* by Don Federico Bordejé. The author acknow-

ledges his debt to the research and lifelong dedication of Mr. Bordejé. The material presented here on the bridges of Alcántara and San Martin, on the castles of Peñafiel, Guadamur, Pedraza, Villaviciosa (Avila), La Mota at Medina del Campo and Arévalo, as well as the plan of Peñafiel, owe a great deal to him.

The castles of Guadalajara have been thoroughly studied by Dr. Francisco Layna Serrano, whose book *Castillos de Guadalajara* has also provided important material for the presentation of castles such as Zorita de los Canes, Atienza, Anguix and Sigüenza included in this book. Dr. Layna Serrano's drawings have also provided certain details for the plans of Zorita de los Canes and Atienza.

One of the most evocative books on Castilian castles is *Castillos de Castilla* by the Count of Gamazo. The author has freely drawn on this book for basic data regarding the important castles of Coca, Cuéllar and Torrelobatón. The distinguished historian of Spanish architecture, Don Vincente Lampérez y Romea continues to provide today one of the most important sources of material on castles. His classic *Arquitectura Civil Española* has been consulted throughout this work. His drawings also, particularly those of Real de Manzanares, Buitrago, La Mota at Medina del Campo and Belmonte are the source of the plans of these castles included in this book.

One castle that has long defied the efforts of many serious students of Spanish religious and military architecture is Turégano. The record has finally been put straight by Don Eugenio Colorado y Laca and by Father Plácido Centeno, the present vicar of Turégano. I owe to Don Angel Dotor information regarding a publication by the latter, which stresses the importance of the religious origin of Turégano and its subsequent transformation into a castle.

It is the author's hope that if his book has any merit the debt owed to the Spanish authors who have preceded him is clearly expressed, since it is considerable. He also wishes to express here his admiration for the superb verse translation of the Spanish *Cantar de Myo Cid* due to Mr. W. S. Merwin in *The Poem of the Cid*. Portions of Cantos 128 and 136 are quoted in the chapters on the castles of Gormaz and San Servando.

'The house of everyone is to him as his castle and fortress . . .'
Sir Edward Coke (1552–1634)

INTRODUCTION

A castle, from the Latin *castellum* (a diminutive of *castrum*: a fortified place), is defined by Webster as ' a large fortified building or buildings, especially that of a prince or nobleman '. It is, however, really more than that, it is an instrument of war, a tool of conquest, and an element of colonization. These characteristics have nowhere been more evident than in Spain, a country which was ravaged by war for more than 800 years. That Spanish castles are numerous is not surprising—they are a corollary of the historical and social developments, resulting from the Arab invasions that began in the eighth century, and the subsequent lengthy period of the Reconquest. While the old expression ' Castles in Spain ' may seem to convey a dream-like quality, these castles are very real. On the other hand, nothing better characterizes the Iberian temperament than some of these structures—for they are proud and isolated, in the ghostly vigil they have kept for centuries.

More than 2,000 castles and fortified palaces have been built in Spain.[1] Today, only a few have been restored, and the rest are mostly in ruins, in some cases no more than a roofless shell where weeds grow high in the courtyard. It is not only time and the elements that are responsible for their sad state of decay: for political reasons, Queen Isabella of Castile decreed, at the beginning of the sixteenth century, that the fortified palaces owned by the nobility should be demolished. Later, many imposing structures were obliterated by war, particularly during the War of the Spanish Succession (1700–13) and the Napoleonic occupation of 1808-14. Some castles still standing today, like those of Torija, Anguix and Sepúlveda carry scars of these struggles.

Nevertheless, many of Spain's castles have survived all these hazards, even that of human indifference. They stand alone as sombre witnesses to a violent, barbarous, and sometimes glorious past. Like gigantic molars from the calcinated jaws of the earth, to use Ortega y Gasset's expression, the castles are symbols that each man must decipher alone. It is with these magnificent relics that this book is concerned.

[1] Sarthou Carreres, in *Castillos de España*, lists a total of 1,612. The Asociación de Amigos de los Castillos and the Patronato Nacional have catalogued 10,000 castles, walled cities and fortified enclosures, of which 14% have no titular owner.

SPAIN AND ISLAM

At the beginning of the eighth century, Spain, which had undergone successive invasions by Phoenicians, Greeks, Carthaginians, Romans and Visigoths, was also weakened by internal revolts. It was a Catholic country, the Visigothic King Reccared having announced his conversion to the faith more than a century before, in the year 589. The capital was Toledo. In 710, a new wave of invaders—the Arabs—were preparing an assault, and that year marked the first Arab reconnaissance in the south of Spain near Tarifa. In 711 an army estimated at 12,000, consisting mostly of Berber warriors, landed in Spain under the command of Tarik the One-Eyed. This was a new stage in the plan of conquest preached by Mohammed with the purpose of converting all of mankind to the new faith. In little less than a century since Mohammed's death in 632, Islam had over-run Palestine, Persia, Egypt and the whole of North Africa. Spain and all Christian Europe were to be the next stage.

At the time of the Arab invasion the Visigothic King, Roderic, was occupied in putting down a revolt in the Basque countries. He hastened south and met his enemy near Jerez de la Frontera, at a place traditionally located on the banks of the Guadalete River. The encounter there lasted seven days and Roderic, weakened by the defection of some of his troops to Tarik, was defeated. Through this one battle the Visigothic kingdom of Spain was destroyed, and the whole peninsula was laid open to Arab incursion.

In the next two decades the Infidels conquered all the lands south of the Pyrenees, except for Galicia and the Asturias on the north-western corner of the peninsula, where fog and rain stopped their fanatical advance. However, the Moslem raiders, undeterred, continued their march across the mountains, and penetrated deep into the country of the Franks. By 720 they had occupied Narbonne and were besieging Toulouse. Even these advances were but preliminary steps. In 729, when a distinguished leader named Abd-ar-Rahman was appointed to govern the recently conquered Spain, the Arabs began preparations for the complete conquest of Gaul. In the summer of 732 he crossed the Pyrenees at the head of an army 80,000 strong. The mediaeval chroniclers, although humble monks writing in the peace of their monasteries, were able to convey the terror that the Moslem invasion caused among the inhabitants of the regions south of the Loire. It was to be Charles Martel, son of Pepin of Heristal and Duke of the Austrasian Franks, who finally managed to stop the Arab invaders in the vicinity of Tours in 732. Contemporary chroniclers recorded the invasion and its ultimate defeat in vivid language: 'Then Abd-ar-Rahman, seeing the land filled with the multitude of his army, pierces through the mountains, tramples over rough and level ground, plunders far into the country of the Franks and smites all with the sword . . . While he strives to spoil and burn the holy shrine of Tours, he encounters the chief of the Austrasian Franks, Charles, a man of war since his youth. There, for nearly seven days they strive intensely, and at last they set themselves in battle array; and the nations of the North standing firm as a wall, and impenetrable as a zone of ice, utterly slay the Arabs with the edge of the sword.' [1]

[1] Sir Edward S. Creasy: *Fifteen Decisive Battles of the World*. London, 1851.

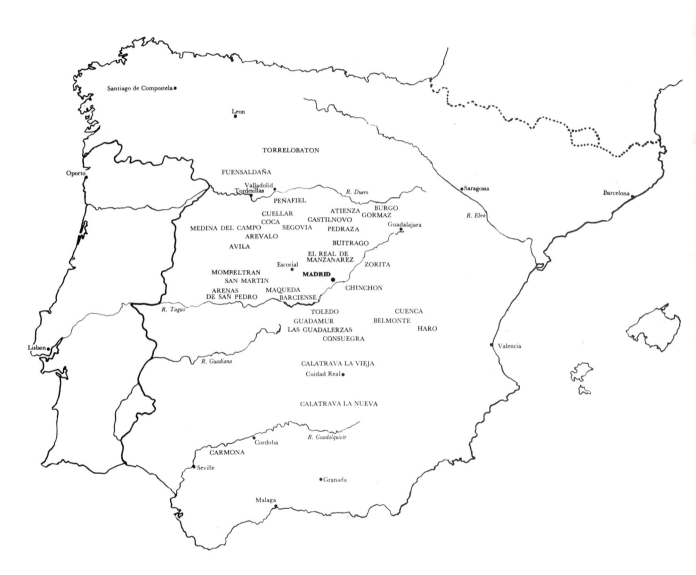

Santiago de Compostela •

Leon •

Oporto •

TORRELOBATON

FUENSALDAÑA
Valladolid
Tordesillas   *R. Duero*

PEÑAFIEL   BURGO
                          ATIENZA GORMAZ
CUELLAR
        COCA   CASTILNOVO   • Saragossa
MEDINA DEL CAMPO SEGOVIA PEDRAZA   Guadalajara •
        AREVALO   *R. Ebro*
        AVILA   BUITRAGO

                EL REAL DE
                MANZANAREZ
        Escorial •   ZORITA
MOMBELTRAN   **MADRID** •
SAN MARTIN
ARENAS   MAQUEDA   CHINCHON
DE SAN PEDRO BARCIENSE

        R. Tagus
                        TOLEDO   CUENCA
                GUADAMUR   BELMONTE
                LAS GUADALERZAS   HARO
                CONSUEGRA

        R. Guadiana

                CALATRAVA LA VIEJA
                Cuidad Real •

                CALATRAVA LA NUEVA

Lisbon •

                        R. Guadalquivir
        • Cordoba
CARMONA
        • Seville   • Granada

        Malaga •

Barcelona •

Valencia •

1 5

[2] Madrid, 1820.

Returning from the battle of Tours (or Poitiers, as many historians prefer to identify it), Abd-ar-Rahman was mortally wounded in a surprise attack. His army, utterly defeated, withdrew rapidly towards their bases in southern France, and the Moslem dream of the conquest of all Christendom was crushed. The battle of Tours marked the limit of Arab penetration into Western Europe. It is fascinating to compare the accounts of Christian chroniclers with those of their Arab counterparts. Don José Antonio Conde in *Historia de la dominación de los Arabes en España*,[2] compiled these Arab sources which, although differing in many details from those of the Christians, agreed on the tremendous defeat that was suffered by the invaders. Tours was indeed a turning point in the history of Europe. Sir Edward S. Creasy includes in his book *Fifteen Decisive Battles of the World*, the following translation of the Arab version compiled by Conde: 'Near the river Owar (probably Loire) the two great hosts of the two languages and the two creeds were set against each other. The hearts of Abd-ar-Rahman, his captains and his men were filled with wrath and pride, and they were the first to begin to fight. The Moslem horsemen dashed fierce and frequent forward against the battalions of the Franks, who resisted manfully, and many fell dead on either side, until the going down of the sun. Night parted the two armies but in the grey of the morning the Moslems returned to the battle. Their cavaliers had soon hewn their way into the centre of the Christian host.'

'But many of the Moslems were fearful for the safety of the spoils they had stored in their tents, and a false cry arose in their ranks that some of the enemy were plundering the camp; whereupon several squadrons of the Moslem horsemen rode off to protect their tents. But it seemed as if they fled and all the host was troubled. And while Abd-ar-Rahman strove to check their tumult, and to lead them back to battle, the warriors of the Franks came around him, and he was pierced through with many spears so that he died. Then all the host fled before the enemy, and many died in the flight. This deadly defeat of the Moslems, and the loss of the great leader and good cavalier, Abd-ar-Rahman, took place in the 115th year [of the Hegira, or flight of Mohammed from Mecca to Medina, 622 A.D.].'

16

The Moslem wave then withdrew, but its power was not permanently broken. For three decades the Arabs occupied parts of southern France, even managing to conquer Avignon in 737. Only with the reconquest by the Franks of their base at Narbonne in 759 were the Arabs finally deprived of their foothold in Gaul. In the Iberian Peninsula, on the other hand, the Moslem wave settled itself firmly. It was here, in the country that the Arabs called Al-Andalus, that their civilization was destined to leave its mark for ever.

The Arab occupation of Spain never knew peace. Equally fanatic, and supported by the clergy, the remainder of Christian Spain that had found refuge in Galicia and the Asturias eventually started their slow descent towards the South. Led by a living legend, King Pelayo, the Christian Reconquest began with the victory of Covadonga in 718. It then took 200 years for the Christians to reach the Duero River at Peñafiel, a distance of no more than 130 miles as the crow flies. The war went back and forth for two more centuries before the country between the Duero and the Tagus could be secured.

Peñafiel: the keep seen from the first inner bailey.

The building of castles and walled cities followed closely upon the movement of the armies. The Arabs built Gormaz, Calatrava la Vieja and Buitrago, which were all classical *alcazabas* meant for war, and were very different from the later fortress-palaces in Andalucia. The Christians also built strongholds, sometimes on older foundations of Roman, Visigothic or Arab origin, adapting them to incorporate

Calatrava La Nueva: entrance to the castle hall.

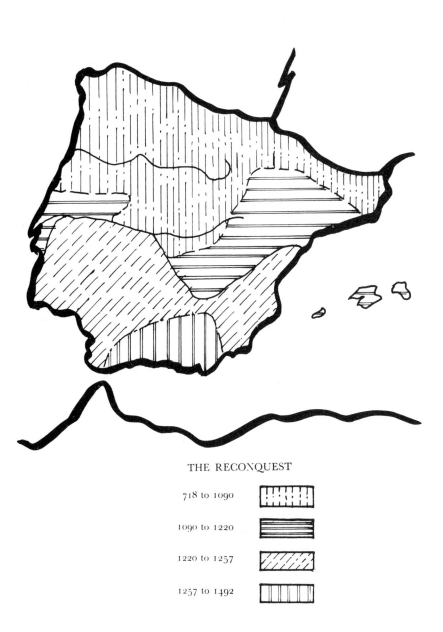

THE RECONQUEST

718 to 1090

1090 to 1220

1220 to 1257

1257 to 1492

improvements learned from their experiences in the Crusades. Slowly the Arab supremacy, which had been based on a sophisticated knowledge of the arts of war and peace, gave way in the face of a determined enemy supported by the rest of Europe.

The period between the end of the eleventh century and the beginning of the thirteenth saw tremendous changes in the structure

of both Christian and Moslem power in the Peninsula. The Caliphate of Córdoba, proclaimed by Abd-ar-Rahman III in the year 929, was for a whole century perhaps the most enlightened state in western Europe. The city of Córdoba had at that time a population of 500,000 and was the most populous centre of Europe after Constantinople. However, internal dissension was undermining the Caliphate. By 1031 it had ceased to exist, giving way to a conglomeration of minor states called *taifas*, ruled by Arab chieftains of dubious status. The reconquest of Toledo in 1085, by King Alfonso VI, threatened the very life of these fragments of Al-Andalus. The danger became so acute that an embassy representing the chieftains of major cities such as Seville, Córdoba and Granada went to Africa to ask for help from the powerful Berber empire of the Almorávides or Murabits (hermits). In 1086 help came in the form of a seemingly invincible force headed by Yusef-ibn-Tashfin, and later by his son Ali, which not only defeated Alfonso VI, the crowned King of León and Castile in a series of battles culminating at Uclés in 1108, but also wiped out the weak *taifa*

kingdoms. Moslem Spain was united again, and had become a part of the Almoravid empire, with Córdoba as its capital.

Within three decades, however, this apparently united state was weakened by internal friction and by the softening of the Berber's ascetic spirit in the sensuous climate of Al-Andalus. The deterioration was so pronounced that Alfonso VII of Castile was able to take

Córdoba in 1147 and to sack Granada and Seville. The defeat of Islam was averted for a second time by the emergence of another fanatical sect, the Almohades or Unitarians, who landed in Spain in 1146 and gradually proceeded to reconquer the areas lost by the Almorávides. By 1195, the Almohades, whose capital was in Morocco, had kept control of Moslem Spain for almost half a century. That year the Almohade Emperor Yacub inflicted a tremendous blow on Alfonso VIII of Castile at the battle of Alarcos, where the king himself sought unsuccessfully to die among his thousands of dead. Alfonso never forgot the last minute withdrawal of his allies, León and Navarre, and when he was ready to fight again he obtained a call to Crusade from Pope Innocent III. The reaction was encouraging and, by the beginning of 1212, an imposing army estimated at 60,000 knights was assembled in Toledo. From there the most important Christian army ever gathered in Spain moved ponderously southward. Yacub, the victor of Alarcos, had been succeeded by his son, the Caliph Mohammed-al-Nazir, who took up his position at Las Navas de Tolosa. At this

Montealegre: elaborate corbelling and stylised machicolations above the main gate.

point south of the Sierra Morena, he awaited the Christian attack with 100,000 mounted men in line formation strongly backed by infantry. In the centre stood a palisade, bound with heavy chains, where Mohammed placed himself. When the Christians attacked, they fought in single combat rather than as a body. The Moslems began to lose ground on their flanks; but in the centre, a strong band of their war-

Montealegre: entrance gate and door to the keep from the courtyard.

Tordesillas: view across the Duero River.

riors destroyed the élite force of the Knights of Calatrava and almost carried the day. They were only prevented by the incredible resilience of the Christian infantry supported by the Knights of Santiago.

This classic mediaeval battle showed for the first time the value of spearmen on foot, for they managed to resist the heavily mounted Saracen knights. Indeed it can be said that the Spanish infantry was born at Las Navas de Tolosa. They became eventually the famous *Tercios* who dominated Europe centuries later, and were destined to uphold the power of imperial Spain, and their own reputation of invincibility, for more than 150 years, from the beginning of the sixteenth century until their defeat at Rocroi in the seventeenth century.

On the battlefield of Las Navas de Tolosa, Mohammed knew that his great opportunity had been lost when the stockade was reached by the Christian right flank under King Sancho V of Navarre. The Arab king then retreated with his bodyguard towards Baeza while his warriors, leaderless, were left to die. Contemporary chronicles estimate Moslem losses at 125,000. Even if the figure was exaggerated, it deserves respect. There is no question that the Arabs paid a tremendous price in this battle and that it sealed their fate in the Peninsula. The Reconquest was assured on that day, July 16, 1212, and the Church was to commemorate it through the centuries as The Day of Triumph of the Cross. Alfonso VIII, too, could proudly hang the Moslem standard, blue with stars of gold, the symbol of his victory,

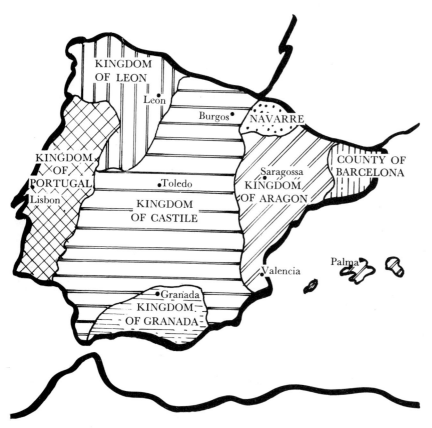

THE IBERIAN PENINSULA IN THE 13th CENTURY

from the vaults of Toledo's Cathedral.

It was almost three centuries, however, before the Moorish kingdom of Granada finally surrendered in 1492. This delay, considering that Al-Andalus never recovered from Las Navas de Tolosa, can only be explained in terms of a parallel development: the struggle for the unification of the three kingdoms of Castile, León and Aragón into one nation. León was reunited with Castile in 1230 under Ferdinand III and final unity was achieved by the marriage of Isabella of Castile to Ferdinand of Aragón in 1469, followed by her coronation in Segovia as 'Queen proprietor' (*reina propietaria*) of Castile on December 13, 1474. The fall of the last strongholds of Arab power in Spain began in 1482, when their Catholic majesties attacked Alhama, deep in the

heart of Moorish territory. Finally, in the Spring of 1490, Ferdinand marched with a strong force into the cultivated plains or *vega* of Granada. The formal siege of the well-defended city itself, which had at the time a population of 200,000, began in April 1491. It lasted until November, when the capitulation of Granada was agreed upon. The keys of the city were delivered on January 2, 1492 by Abdallah, the last Nazarite king of Granada, to Ferdinand and Isabella. This action ended the long march that had begun at Covadonga in the year 718.

The year 1492 was called the *annus mirabilis*, the year of the miracles, because in addition to the successful completion of the Reconquest, it witnessed the 'discovery' of America by Christopher Columbus.

Another fateful event was to take place the same year: the expulsion of the Jews, who were forced to scatter and settle in the Mediterranean regions.

The year 1492 was indeed the end of the Middle Ages. In the Iberian Peninsula the closing of this historic period also marked the conclusion of the great cycle of construction of Spanish castles and fortified palaces.

Following in the footsteps of previous builders, such as the ancient Iberians who erected the cyclopean walls of Tarragona, and the Romans who built imposing fortified camps like Borja and Numantia, the Arab invaders brought with them their own art of fortification. When the decline of the caliphate of Córdoba began in the tenth century, their fortified enclosures or *alcazabas* were already spread over a great part of Spain. On the Mediterranean coast, for example, Málaga and Almería had their powerful *alcazabas*, still imposing today; in fact Málaga, with its three enceintes and the inter-connecting

Torrelobatón: detail of the keep.

26

alcazabas of Gibralfaro, constituted one of the most highly-developed defence systems in Europe in the tenth century. In the hinterland the Arabs built thousands of strongholds, many of which were subsequently used as the foundations for Christian castles. Their concept was simple: an irregular wall of enceinte, reinforced by square or polygonal towers. The main building material was usually a mixture of cement and pebbles or stones poured between two boards and left to dry in the sun. After a time, the boards were removed to expose extremely strong walls. This system of construction, called *tapia*, was preferred by the Arabs to all others, even those employing stone or brick. As a result, Moorish masons kept the square or polygonal lay-out for their towers, as it was perfectly adapted to *tapia* construction, and seldom used the round tower favoured by the Christians in their castles.

In the Arabs' *alcazabas*, the wall of enceinte, usually crenellated with typical pointed merlons, protected a conglomeration of buildings erected against the enclosing wall or sometimes grouped around a well. In other cases, such as in the original Arab stronghold at Calatrava la Vieja, a mosque was the main feature within the fortified enclosure. Not unreasonably, these *alcazabas*, because of their apparent freedom of lay-out, have been compared to oases. They were built for garrison purposes and were pure instruments of war. Gormaz on the Duero River, with walls almost a mile long and supported by twenty-one square towers, still bears witness today to the Arabs' aptitude as builders. Built in the tenth century, Gormaz was far more advanced than any known contemporary castles in Europe. Even the ' motte-and-bailey' type, which appeared in Normandy and other parts of the Continent in the middle of the eleventh century, were mainly timber constructions, while Gormaz was built of excellent ashlar stone.

The earliest examples of Moslem fortified structures in the Peninsula are to be found in Andalucía, the southern portion of Spain whose name derives from the Arab name of *Al-Andalus*. In this area, the walls and towers of Seville, as well as the powerful fortress of Carmona, and that of Alcalá de Guadaira, which defend Seville from the north and south-east, have preserved, in spite of later Christian restoration, important features of their original Moslem design. Carmona, for example, still has the beautiful Moorish gate of its *alcazaba* with the remains of perfect machicolations. While Alcalá de Guadaira, which was conquered in 1246 by Ferdinand III of Castile, is, in spite of fifteenth-century restoration by the Marquis of Cadiz, one of the most impressive ruins in Al-Andalus. Its wall of enceinte was supported by eight towers; one of these, defending the gate, was set apart from the wall and connected to it by a bridge. We shall see later on how this extramural tower, known in Spanish as *torre albarrana*, became a feature of some of the castles built by the Spanish Military Orders. Other typically Spanish contributions to the art of fortification, such as pentagonal towers to protect poorly defended spots, and *corachas* or cutting walls which divided the attacking forces into separate sectors, were also adopted from the Moslem enemies.

The Arabs continued to use their typical square-tower design in *alcázars* as well as in their castle-palaces. The latter, often built of stone, developed during the thirteenth and fourteenth centuries from the early *alcazabas*. They marked the highest point in Arab architecture in Spain and are among the great monuments of Europe. Almodóvar de Rio in the province of Córdoba, today carefully rebuilt, is a fine example: it stands inaccessible behind high crenellated walls on the banks of the Guadalquivir River.

Unlike the disordered lay-out of the *alcazabas*, which were purely functional instruments of war, the Arab castle-palaces show a clearly aesthetic approach in their construction. The best illustration of this development is the Alhambra of Granada. Known towards the end of the ninth century as an *alcazaba* under the name Calat Alhamra (the red castle), it was expanded in the thirteenth century by King Mohammed-ben-Alhamar, who transformed it into the most famous *alcázar* of all Al-Andalus.

Carmona: detail of the machicolations above the city gate.

SPAIN AND EUROPE

The Christian art of military fortification attained, too, an impressive level of achievement in Spain. Castles such as Calatrava la Nueva, Peñafiel and La Mota of Medina del Campo are among the most imposing in Europe. However, these castles had evolved from the concepts of fortification which had been applied since the early stages of the Reconquest. The primitive Christian castle of the tenth century relied on the strength of the main tower, and the lay-out was adapted to the topography of the ground. It stood generally on a hill and its walls were in some cases integrated with those of the town. The main building materials were bricks and stone rubble. When the Christians conquered a Moslem redoubt, they usually added their own type of strong tower, with access normally on the second floor, to the extended walls of the Arab *alcazaba*. This main tower became known as the *torre del homenaje* (tower of homage), a term which is still in current usage. It was, in a way, the equivalent of the English keep or French donjon, which served both as the residence of the feudal Master and as the castle's ultimate defence. However, in Spain, castles were used originally for garrison purposes and, even after the Reconquest, they seldom or never became truly residential. The feudal system as it was known in other parts of Europe, never reigned supreme in Spain, although the nobility tried to implement it under the House of Trasta-mara in the fourteenth and fifteenth centuries. A factor that helped to prevent the spread of feudalism was the granting of *fueros*, or charters of rights and obligations, to the inhabitants of Spanish towns, parti-cularly those recently reconquered or resettled. Since the *fueros* defined the relationship of the individual and of the town to the local overlord, they introduced a third factor in the struggle between the kings and the nobility. The freedom of the people became a political issue (wisely manipulated by the Crown), and one which naturally functioned to the detriment of the powerful overlords. Thus contained, the nobility owned very few castles until the fifteenth century. This situation explains also why Spanish military architecture in the fourteenth century seems to have stopped evolving at a relatively early stage—usually with the keep-and-courtyard type of the castle of enceinte. In Western Europe this type of castle had several layers of defences, with crenellated walls of different heights protecting the main tower or keep. Since this was a passive concept of defence, the keep had to be placed as far as possible from the entrance of the castle. Château Gaillard, built in France in 1196–8 by Richard Coeur-de-Lion, was a perfect example. Strategically located on a site controlling the Seine valley, it was considered impregnable. Its defences included an extensive barbican or forework, and two imposing walls of enceinte. However, Château Gaillard was taken in 1214 by a group of attackers who peeled off the layers of defence like an onion and forced the ex-posed keep to surrender.

As a result of experiences such as this, the classic idea of the keep-and-courtyard or bailey type of castle was replaced in certain European countries towards the middle of the thirteenth century by a very different concept: that of the fortified gate, which protected the approach to the castle. Less than a century later another type of castle

La Mota, Medina del Campo: a section of the curtain wall showing the masonry bridge which spans the moat, and the keep.

appeared on the Continent and in the British Isles. In these the keep was moved forward to combine with the strongest point of defence, which was now at the entrance. These developments had little impact in Spain, although the fortified gatehouse is found in La Mota, which was built around the year 1479. It is a powerful feature that reminds

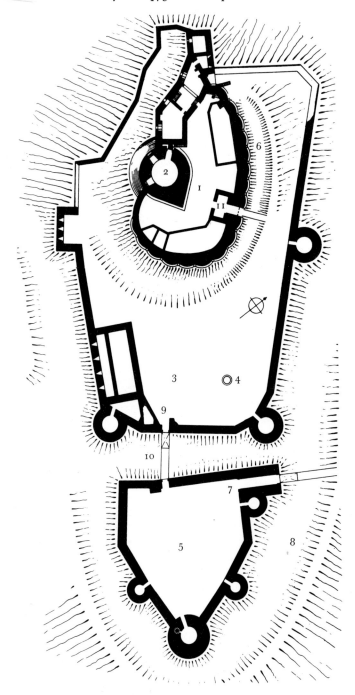

us of the gatehouse at the castle of Stirling in Scotland; however, La Mota's gatehouse is relatively modest when compared with those of the Welsh castles built two centuries earlier, in the time of Edward I.

An important stage in the evolution of European castles was the disappearance of the keep, which was replaced by a symmetrical

CHATEAU GAILLARD

1 Inner Bailey
2 Donjon
3 Middle Bailey
4 Well
5 Outer Bailey
6 Moat
7 Outer Gate
8 Moat
9 Middle Gate
10 Bridge
11 Inner Gate

disposition of twin gatehouses and towers, as at Beaumaris Castle in Wales (1295), or by a frontal gatehouse and relatively modest curtain walls, as in the castle of Doune in Scotland (mid-fourteenth century). But these innovations did not leave their mark on the development of Spanish military architecture.

Other concepts, such as the use of symmetry as a major planning tool in the design of castles, were clearly adopted in Spain. Symmetrical structures were built in the fourteenth and fifteenth centuries, following the previously mentioned European examples such as Beaumaris and the rigorously geometrical Castel del Monte in Southern Italy, built by Frederick II toward the second half of the thirteenth century. Spanish ingenuity of design was shown in the star-shaped castle of Belmonte in the province of Cuenca and even more so in the circular castle of Bellver on the island of Mallorca. Symmetry was also an important element in those castle-palaces built on the plains of Castile, such as Fuensaldaña. But the crowning achievement of this trend which will be mentioned later, was the castle-palace of Coca, in the province of Segovia.

The Spaniards were perhaps so attached to the proud symbol of the *torre del homenaje* that they did not want to relinquish it. In general, Christian castles in the Peninsula retained the keep and the corresponding inner and outer wards or baileys, called in Spanish *patio de armas*. Among these castles, few reached the perfection of Peñafiel on the Duero River. Peñafiel was built in the middle of the fifteenth century on the crest of a hill, and its two walls of enceinte are still standing today. There are also two well-defined wards, the inner one enclosing the massive keep.

A strong outer gate is protected by twin towers on either side, a moat, and machicolations above the door. A second gate, defended

Belmonte: remains of the gatehouse and, beyond, the path leading to the town.

by corbelled projections, opens into the outer bailey. When the visitor reaches it, he is still a long way from the entrance to the keep: first there is a moat running across the width of the outer ward—it has the same function as the moat that defends access to the inner ward at Conway Castle in Wales—the next obstacle is a door, protected by a gun-port, in the wall that divides the enclosure into two wards in the shape of irregular triangles. Once inside the inner ward, you can see the keep with its massive, twelve-foot thick walls. The entrance was through a door at second floor level, which could only be reached by a removeable bridge. Access to the hall was through a typical dog's-leg passage covered by a gun-loop.

Pedraza: a section of the outer ramparts.

Peñafiel is a precursor of the castle-palaces which made their appearance in Spain in the fifteenth century. These, while incorporating the earlier type of defences—crenellated walls, machicolations, arrow and gun-loops—paid greater attention to the refinements of living. Peñafiel's superb keep was built at that time. Many other castles were built as a result of the feudal struggles during the reigns of John II (1406–54) and Henry IV (1454–74). The majority of the new structures retained the keep, as for example Coca, Real de Manzanares and Torrelobatón; but in others it disappeared, as in the castle of Alburquerque, where it became one of the corner towers.

At the beginning of the sixteenth century the impact of the Renaissance on the taste of the tremendously wealthy noblemen and prelates became apparent in the final stage of the development of castle-palaces. An example is La Calahorra near Guadix in the province of Granada, built in 1509–12 by Lorenzo Vásquez of Segovia and the Genoese architect and sculptor Michele Carlone for Don Rodrigo de Vivar y Mendoza, one of the two legitimized sons of the Cardinal Primate of Spain, Don Pedro de Mendoza. La Calahorra seems strangely out of place in sunny Andalucía: its massive towers give the impression of a solid, squat fortress defending its grim interior from men and light. But surprisingly, its powerful exterior hides graceful rooms in a cool marmoreal Italianate style. In this remarkable building the military details have lost their *raison d'être* and become

TORRELOBATON

1 Hall of Keep
2 Inner Ward

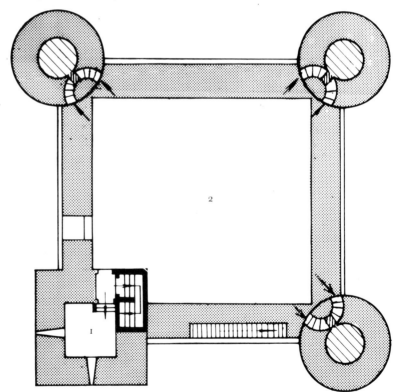

merely decorative. La Calahorra forms a link with the urban palaces of the sixteenth and seventeenth centuries. It also marks the end of the era of the Spanish castle-palace which had begun around the year 1400 on the plains of Castile. In little more than a century, a number of impressive buildings had been created that have an important place in the history of the military architecture of Europe.

BASIC STAGES IN
SPANISH
CASTLE BUILDING

We can establish at this point a certain chronology in the development of Christian castles in Spain. Two major types have been mentioned: castles and castle-palaces, classified according to their main basic function—as instruments of war, or as fortified residences of kings and nobility. This simplified classification may be subdivided by comparing the process of castle building in Christian Spain with that in France. In France there were three basic types of castle:

a) Structures like Château Gaillard, built in the late twelfth century, which had the purely functional purpose of defending the frontiers of the realm.

b) Those castles, such as Coucy, built around 1230, which were also conceived basically as weapons of defence, but which extended their walls of enceinte to protect a town or village, thus introducing a civil factor.

c) The royal castles dating from the early part of the fourteenth century, of which the Château de Vincennes is typical, where an attempt was made to make the living quarters habitable and more attractive.

The development of castle building in Christian Spain had some points in common with that in France. The first stage includes the castles of the Military Orders: Calatrava la Nueva, Zorita de los Canes, the original castle of Anguix in Guadalajara, and Consuegra in the province of Toledo, all dating from the late twelfth or thirteenth centuries. These castles were military in character and strategically located to protect the advance of the Reconquest.

In the second stage, from the late thirteenth to the end of the fourteenth centuries, the castles with their extended walls became the main protection of important centres. During this period the Castilians built the stronghold of Atienza in the province of Soria, the original castle of La Mota of Medina del Campo, Portillo in the province of Valladolid, Torija in Guadalajara, and expanded the Moorish castle of Buitrago in the province of Madrid. They also developed the great *alcázar* of Segovia. In France this second stage marked the supremacy of the monarchy, which was secured after the battle of Bouvines in 1214; but in Spain this new type of castle indicated the end of an immediate Arab threat and the beginning of the nobles' supremacy.

The third stage is that of the castle-palaces, which became in the fifteenth century the concrete expression of the ascendancy of the clergy and nobility in turbulent Spain. Fuensaldaña, Torrelobatón, Villalonso and many others reflected their power. In some cases the builders of castles found, in agreement with Italian trends, a strong appeal in comfort and even luxury. The extensive ruins of Escalona in the province of Toledo, another castle-palace of great merit, illustrate the firm establishment, in the first half of the fifteenth century, of

Torija: view of part of the castle and keep showing the results of El Empecinado's attempt to blow it up during the Napoleonic War. Restoration of the castle had not been completed when this photograph was taken and is only apparent in the false machicolations on the left.

civilian features in heavily defended enclosures. In most cases, the castle-palaces had a symmetrical design, conditioned by the availability of appropriate terrains. *Mudéjar* influence was very strong at this time, as shown in the exteriors of those castles which were built of brick. So, too, the interior décor of the Spanish fifteenth-century castle-palaces was, practically without exception, influenced by Moslem artisans and *Mudéjar* working techniques. In Escalona, for example, an ancient curtain wall, strongly protected by a moat and square towers, created a vast irregular enclosure on a steep hill overlooking the Alberche River. The enclosure in turn was divided into two wards by another moat. The palace, which occupied the inner ward, had a perfectly square lay-out and was decorated with remarkable stucco work of late Gothic design with a *Mudéjar* treatment.

While the process of castle building in Spain may have points in common with the French pattern, a closer analysis of many outstanding Spanish castles reminds us of examples in Great Britain. This is not surprising since the British Isles also played a part in the history of the Spanish Reconquest, as well as in the internal feuding in Spain in the fourteenth century. Sir James Douglas, for example, died near Teba in 1330 while fighting at the head of a battalion of Scottish knights against the Moors. This was the historic occasion when 'the Good Sir James carried the heart of Robert the Bruce in a casket around his neck and fell with the war cry of his clan: "A Douglas!" on his lips'[3]. And Edward the Black Prince, Governor of the English territories in

Escalona: part of the courtyard and ruins of the main tower.

[3] 'He was killed in Spain trying to bring his master's heart to greater glory' says J. D. Mackie in *A History of Scotland*, 1964.

Torrelobatón: one of the corner towers.

south-west France, crossed the Pyrenees in 1367 to support Peter the Cruel in the fight for the Castilian throne with Henry of Trastamara. After Edward's victory at Nájera, Peter presented him with a great ruby, which later became the central jewel in the English Crown of State.

The Conway-Peñafiel line of comparison seems to complete its circle at Escalona. The basic fortifications are still standing: a strong curtain-wall, the moat dividing the enclosure into two wards, and the keep (now transformed into a superb *Mudéjar*-Gothic structure). The main development can be summarized in one word: comfort. Kings had changed and so did their courts. Dr Lampérez, undoubtedly a

Mombeltrán: a corner tower.

highly respected Spanish authority in the field of Mediaeval architecture, mentions that King Jaime the Conqueror was forced to share his sleeping quarters with some of his courtiers because of the inadequate space allowed for human comfort in the early keeps. However, they were not used as permanent residences and their normal garrisons must have been small. By the end of the Middle Ages the keep had been transformed into rich living quarters and the *patio de armas* had become a courtyard with a gallery surrounding it. Nevertheless, these castle-palaces were not permanently used by their Masters and some of them, like Fuensaldaña, show no signs whatever of having been used as dwellings.

In the fifteenth century the rising power of the nobility expressed itself in ambitious architectural projects controlled by families such as those of Pacheco, Fonseca, Mendoza, Carrillo, and Vivero, as well as the great favourite of John II, Don Alvaro de Luna. Towards 1450 the construction of the castle-palaces reached its zenith. But the growing political unity of Spain under Ferdinand and Isabella soon brought about the decline of the nobility. This, and the flowering of the Italian Renaissance (exemplified in La Calahorra), finally brought to an end the era of the castle-palace. By the middle of the sixteenth century, abandonment of those structures which had not already been dismantled by royal command, was widespread, as the patrician families began to build purely civilian palaces to replace them.

Earlier, during the twelfth, thirteenth and fourteenth centuries, the power of the Military Orders was paramount. Few original structures have survived from that period, although many castles of a later date incorporated some elements of their basic structural design. Among those that have survived, Calatrava la Nueva has already been mentioned. This castle, built by the Order of Calatrava c.1216, is a typical example of the tremendous skill developed by the monastic-military orders founded in Spain on similar lines to those of the Templar and Hospitaler Orders. Both the latter were created in Palestine during the Crusades, and had fought in the Peninsula in the twelfth century in the Holy War against the Arabs. They brought

with them building techniques that made an impressive impact on the country and influenced others, such as the Knights of Calatrava, who had the requisite wealth, to use it constructively. Calatrava la Nueva enclosed within its strong walls of enceinte not only a keep, in the traditional manner, but also a convent for the monk-warriors of the Order and a chapel, an excellent example of early Gothic architecture in Spain. Equally impressive are two other vast castle-convents, Loarre in the province of Huesca and Ponferrada in León. Both belonged to the Templars. The activities of the Military Orders are of such interest that a chapter of this book is devoted to them. However, the ruins of two castles built by the knights of Calatrava deserve special mention. One is the modest castle of the Order called Calatrava la Vieja, on the marshes of the Guadiana River, and the other is Zorita de los Canes on the Tagus. The first was built on the site of an ancient Arab *alcazaba* and dates from the twelfth century. Zorita was rebuilt about a century later, possibly around 1290. Both now in a sad state of disrepair, they are among the great treasures of Spanish military architecture.

An important subdivision among Spanish military castles are the *castillos roqueros*, built high on top of hills and made almost inaccessible by their skilful siting on the edge of deep ravines or on sheer cliffs. The true *castillos roqueros* were usually of irregular plan and moderate size, such as those of Atienza, Pedraza and Anguix, discussed here.

San Martín de Valdeiglesias: the garden door.

To build on top of imposing hills and make intelligent use of natural barriers were cherished characteristics of Spanish castle building. When these castles attained large proportions they were called of *gran buque*, meaning that they resembled a ship left high and dry on the land. Peñafiel is a perfect example of a castle of *gran buque*; so is the superb Alcázar of Segovia. Another is Almansa in the province of Albacete (Murcia), a castle built on Arab foundations, which belonged to the Templars until 1310. In 1707, during the War of the Spanish Succession, it witnessed a famous battle when the troops of Philip V of Bourbon defeated the Austrian Pretender and secured the Spanish Crown for the Bourbons. Almansa, though larger than the *roquero* castles of Castile, was fundamentally the same: a keep and crenellated curtain wall, adapted to the terrain, which enclosed an inner ward of irrregular shape. Round towers defended the wall, which was not protected by a gate-house or moat.

The basic function of *roquero* castles such as Almansa was to protect the newly reconquered regions from Moorish incursions. Later, a

Torrelobatón: the inner wall-walk and stairway leading into the corner tower. A meurtrière *can be seen above and to the left of the doorway.*

second type of castle appeared on the plains, particularly in Castile. In most cases these castles were built of stone, with strong walls of enceinte supported by massive round towers at the corners and a square or rectangular *torre del homenaje*. Variations on this basic plan included the alternation of square towers with round turrets in the middle of each wall, as in the early fifteenth-century castle of Montealegre, near Palencia.

Like the *roquero* castles, the castles of the plains stand proudly aloof against the flat, ochre landscape, outwardly intact even today. Built in the fourteenth and fifteenth centuries, these fortresses depended on sheer massiveness for their defence. For instance, Torrelobatón, an

impressive castle in the province of Valladolid, was subjected to an intensive artillery siege during the War of the Comunidades in the first part of the sixteenth century, yet cannon-balls hardly marked the walls. Torrelobatón is an example of highly sophisticated construction techniques: as for instance, the placing of the few ventilation slits in the *torre del homenaje*, the sinister *meurtrières*, and the innovation of having a protective parapet with a smooth, curved form instead of crenellations (to prevent the use of grappling irons). This castle, dominating the village of Torrelobatón in hostile splendour, has no equal in Spain today.

Some of these castles were surrounded by deep moats, usually dry, others had a low, squat outer wall of defence, such as Villafuerte in the province of Valladolid. Fuensaldaña (also in Valladolid) and Villalonso in the province of Zamora are also good examples of this type of castle. A later example is Arévalo in the province of Avila, which shows some characteristics of the feudal architecture found in other parts of Europe, in the massive, disproportionate keep—a fortress

Torrelobatón: the keep.

in itself—and a weak, almost puny, wall.

Some Spanish keeps are of considerable size. The keep of Torrelobatón is 130 feet high, while Peñafiel's rises to 112 feet. In general, however, they appear relatively small when compared with important European examples, such as the donjon of Crest in the department of Drôme (155 feet high). The classic keep of Peñafiel, with a rectangular plan measuring 66 by 46 feet, is only approximately half the size of either the Tower of London (118 by 107 feet) or the keep of Colchester in Essex (152 by 111 feet); but it is notable for its elegance, an attribute of many Spanish keeps of the fourteenth and fifteenth centuries.

Spanish keeps and towers were not an early phase in the evolution of fortified tower-houses such as those that appeared in Scotland in the fourteenth century. As a rule, the Spanish built isolated towers as part of their system of defence and observation. They abounded on the Pyrenees, on the Bay of Biscay and on the Mediterranean coast, where the one at Porto Pi remains to this day an excellent example of the trend. In other parts of the Peninsula, particularly in Castile, towers were built, sometimes on Saracen foundations, for observation and communication—usually by smoke signal. Tower-houses are common only in the Basque country, in the Asturias, and in the province of Santander (which, although part of Castile, reaches the Cantabrian coast). Of these structures perhaps the best known is La Torrona in Santander, a fifteenth-century house with defensive hourds. These hourds were timber encasements projecting from the wall-heads of a castle and used to defend it from attack to its walls or gates—a very popular method of defence in the Middle Ages all over Europe.

Peñafiel: view from the west of the castle on its ' faithful rock '.

51

There are scattered examples of tower-houses throughout Spain.
Two of the most interesting are the beautiful Torre del Clavero in
Salamanca, 92 feet high, which was built by Francisco de Sotomayor,
the *clavero* or financial administrator of the Military Order of Alcántara,
and Villarejo de Salvanes in the province of Madrid. The latter had a
low wall of enceinte, probably not very strong, and may have been
originally the keep of the castle.

The emergence of the Spanish castle-palaces in the fifteenth century
was contemporary to the development of artillery and fire-arms as
weapons of siege and defence. Their use in the first half of the fifteenth
century is recorded in accounts of the battles over strongholds such as
Atienza and Torija, as well as during the final stages of the Reconquest.
Mining, however, continued to be of great importance and it is obvious
that, even in the sixteenth century, this method could and did, in many
cases, outshine the actual gun fighting. M. J. Quintana, for example,
in his biography of Don Gonzalo Fernández de Córdoba, the great
military leader of the sixteenth century, devotes many pages to his
feats of arms, including the storming of castles. Typically, **Fernández
de Córdoba**'s conquest in 1501 of the great Italian bastion of Castelnuovo (or Maschio Angioino), an imposing Neapolitan fortress
expanded by the Aragonese monarchy, was accomplished by the use
of powerful mines. So it is important to bear in mind that, while having
abundant gun-loops, Spanish castle-palaces of the fifteenth century

Torrelobatón: detail of a meurtrière *from
inside a corner tower.*

52

also possessed extremely solid walls and widely splayed foundations (or plinths) in order to minimize the impact of cannon balls and prevent the use of mines. One of the best examples of Spanish ingenuity in the design of castles adapted to the use of artillery was the tremendous stronghold of Salses in Rousillon (France) which was built by Ferdinand and Isabella when the area was under Spanish domination in the latter part of the fifteenth century. Its walls, reputed to be 70 feet thick in some parts, are unmatched in the Peninsula, or in Europe for that matter.

Salses, because of its size, cannot be considered indicative of a trend in castle building in Spain in the second part of the fifteenth century. However, certain castle-palaces may be grouped together and called transitional. These structures established a link between the early developments of the fifteenth century (when towers were not yet clearly adapted to the use of cannon) and the military fortresses of the seventeenth, eighteenth and nineteenth centuries. The transitional castles had an unmistakable low, squat shape and walls of exceptional thickness. Their main feature was a large tower, usually disproportionate to the rest of the building, which housed one or more cannon. The castle of Las Navas del Marqués, in the province of Avila, is the classical example of this type of heavily defended nobleman's palace. Las Navas del Marqués and even Salses were conceived years after the Scottish castle of Ravenscraig (Fife), begun in 1460, which was

the first castle to be specifically adapted to artillery defence in Great Britain. In turn, Las Navas, which expressed a Spanish nobleman's desire for comfort and security, was followed by other castles that were clearly designed for the use of cannon. One of them, Grajal de Campos in León, a compact structure with gunports at three levels, was built in the early sixteenth century. A castle of the plain, this was the Castilian equivalent of Ravenscraig and of the later English coastal fortresses built by Henry VIII. The European cycle of artillery castles, originating in 1460 with the Scottish example, may be considered as practically completed by 1542 with the construction by Christian III of Malmöhus, a great castle-palace in Sweden.

Toward the middle of the sixteenth century, castle-palaces ceased to be built in Europe. Their place was taken by palaces which were totally civilian in function, and by forts which were totally military, with living accommodation limited to their garrison. At that time, Spain, under the Hapsburgs, followed a similar course to that of the rest of Europe.

The Walled City of Avila: the San Vicente gate.

54

It was mentioned earlier that walled cities have existed in Spain from very early times. The Arabs were later great builders of military enceintes to protect their towns, particularly in Andalucía. In Castile, the concept of the walled city, best represented by Avila, became of great importance. Avila, a marvel of the Middle Ages almost intact today, is representative of the close contact existing during the Reconquest between the Spanish nobility and their trans-Pyrenean allies: it was the precursor of Carcassonne and Aigues-Mortes in France, Conway in Wales, Dubrovnik in Yugoslavia and Visby in Sweden; but the walls of Avila, with their 88 remarkable towers, make it the most powerful of them all. These ramparts were the product of a long experience of fortification which culminated in the effort made by Raymond of Burgundy (son-in-law of Alfonso VI of Castile) to control the territory north of Toledo after its reconquest in 1085. Avila was not alone: Toledo, Burgos, and Alcalá de Henares also became important walled cities. In fact, dozens of *pueblos* or villages are still walled today, such as the charming Pedraza de la Sierra in the province of Segovia, Olmedo in Valladolid, or even Buitrago, near Madrid, which is built inside and around extensive fortifications of Moorish origin.

It would be beyond the scope of this book to cover all the castles, fortified palaces and walled cities in the different provinces of Spain. Each of these has outstanding examples of military architecture. No region, however, has the concentration of important castles that is found in the two Castiles—la Nueva and la Vieja—particularly in the area between the Duero and Tagus Rivers. This, the historical heart of Spain, is a land of castles. Spaniards have an expression to indicate this wealth of proud fortresses: ' *Para castillos, Castilla* '. And so it is.

Villaviciosa (Avila)

THE PROVINCE OF VALLADOLID

Only Segovia can compare with this province in the profusion and variety of its castles. The river Duero, flowing through Valladolid, was for centuries the frontier between the Christian kingdom of León and the Arab dominions controlled by local chieftains paying allegiance to the Caliphate of Córdoba.

From the first half of the eighth century, when the Reconquest started its long descent from the Asturias towards the South, until the beginning of the eleventh century, when the Christian armies reached the Duero at Peñafiel, three centuries of almost constant warfare elapsed. The struggle was a bloody see-saw, with strongholds changing hands many times, forcing Christians and Moslems alike to increase their garrisons and build additional fortresses. Even when the Duero was finally secured by the Spaniards, almost four centuries passed before the final collapse of the power of Islam in Western Europe.

The Reconquest and the internal struggles of the fifteenth and sixteenth centuries left their marks on the province of Valladolid. The influence of the Crusades in Palestine and the help of the French in fighting the Moors and applying techniques learned in the Holy Land, led to the adaptation of early strongholds into powerful castles with a strong Gothic character. Fuensaldaña, Peñafiel, and La Mota at Medina del Campo, are three of the best preserved examples of military architecture in Spain. Unfortunately others, loaded with history and glory, have disappeared. Among these, none perhaps was more important than Tordesillas. It was here, in September 1520, that the daughter of Isabella of Castile, Joanna the Mad, presided for the only time in her life over the Cortes, the governing body of the kingdom so recently united by her mother. This marked the highest point of the famous War of the Comuneros led by Don Juan de Padilla. The Comuneros were motivated by the nationalistic and democratic ideals of the Spanish populace and supported the just claim of Joanna against Charles V. It was at Tordesillas that the revolt received a vital blow.

Tordesillas, today a sleepy town baking under the implacable Spanish sun, was a powerful bulwark in the Middle Ages. When the city was attacked and besieged by 10,000 seasoned troops in December 1520, almost everybody who was able to fight took his place on the ramparts and put up a courageous resistance to the attackers. The defeat came with a breach or *portillo* in the walls, made by cannon, which allowed the Royalist troops to enter the city and engage in hand to hand fighting in the streets. A contemporary chronicler relates how the victorious soldiers found poor Joanna standing in the courtyard of the palace. They led her back to her room in a state of helpless bewilderment, ' knowing little and caring even less what had happened '.

Peñafiel: general view from the south-west.

56

PEÑAFIEL

The proud castle of Peñafiel (the faithful rock) stands on a hill, dominating the southern banks of the river Duero, halfway between Valladolid and Aranda de Duero. The area, which was of great historical importance during the early stages of the Reconquest, was part of the county of Castile in the tenth century. This fortified territory was then subject to the kingdom of León and had as its

Peñafiel: the inner bailey and keep taken from the southern tower.

Peñafiel: entrance to the castle reached by a plank spanning the moat; on the left is a gun-loop.

capital the town of Burgos, founded on the site of one of the *castella* that gave their name to the county. In 1035 the dependency of León was elevated to the rank of kingdom. This was due mainly to the most forceful of the Counts of Castile, Fernán González, famous for his successful campaigning not only against the Moors, but also against the powerful tutelage of León. It was Fernán González who, in 947, after the victory of Osma against the Arabs, settled and fortified the site of Peñafiel as an advance frontier outpost. The Christian settlement, hotly disputed, was finally conquered by the troops of the dreaded and invincible Al-Mansur (Almanzor) in 995.

Eighteen years later, in 1013, the position was finally reconquered by Sancho García, who built a castle and new walls to protect the strategically-placed hamlet. The legend claims that Sancho, burying his lance on the top of the stony hill, exclaimed: 'From now on, this will be the faithful rock of Castile'. Hence the name of the castle.[1] The present castle is thought to stand on the site of the old fortress of Sancho García. Parts of it were built at the beginning of the fourteenth century by Don Juan Manuel, a scholar not totally averse to the adventures of war and one of the early masters of Castilian prose.

The Infante Don Manuel, brother of King Alfonso X, the Learned, received the fief of Peñafiel from a relative, the future King Sancho IV of Navarre, as a present for his newly born son, Juan Manuel.

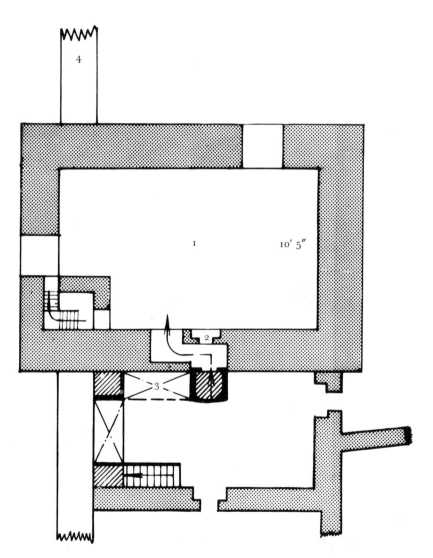

PEÑAFIEL   The Keep
1 Hall
2 Gun-port
3 Bridge
4 Curtain Wall

Around 1307, Don Juan Manuel began building the walls of a new castle, which is considered to be the origin of the present castle of Peñafiel.[2] A typical example of the bumptious Castilian noble, Don Juan Manuel challenged the power of the Castilian crown in the person of Alfonso XI, whom he had good reason to hate, the latter having repudiated his daughter Constance in spite of a marriage con-

[1] The Count of Gamazo mentions in *Castillos en Castilla* that fifty years later the original castle of Peñafiel may have witnessed the meeting of Ferdinand I and the Cid to decide on the opening of their campaign in Portugal that was to end with the reconquest of Coimbra.

[2] As Federico Bordejé indicates in *Castles Itinerary in Castile*, Don Juan Manuel had two castles at Peñafiel. The one in which he lived with his court was later integrated with the Dominican Monastery of San Pablo and it should not be confused with the present castle of Peñafiel. The Infante was buried in this monastery, later transformed into the church of San Pablo. His grave, according to Gamazo, is in the main chapel and is marked by a simple inscription.

tract. Eventually the Infante's castle was demolished in around 1431, by order of King John II.

Peñafiel belonged later to Don Pedro Girón, Master of the Order of Calatrava. He rebuilt the castle in the middle of the fifteenth century, but certain portions, particularly the battlements of the elegant keep, were left unfinished due to his death in 1466.

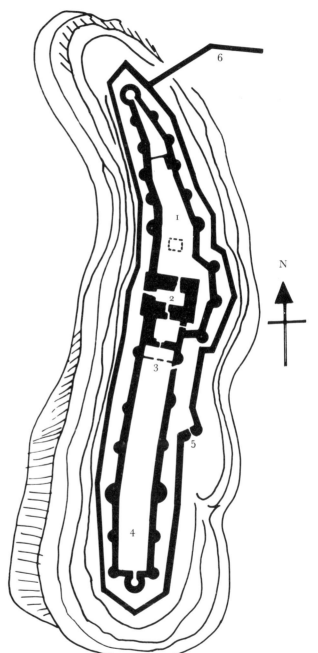

PEÑAFIEL   Ground Plan
(*From F. Bordeje's* Castles Itinerary in Castile)

1 Inner Ward
2 Keep
3 Moat
4 Outer Ward
5 Gate
6 Town Wall

N

Built of ashlar stone and shaped like a vessel riding waves of rock, the castle of Peñafiel was conceived as a refuge in time of war and it is doubtful whether the Master of Peñafiel would have lived there normally. As Federico Bordejé suggests, it is highly unlikely that the Queen of Navarre gave birth to the future Prince of Viana in the keep of Peñafiel in 1421. In spite of a certain residential character, the out-

Peñafiel: a section of the keep showing unfinished machicolations; above the entrance is the coat-of-arms of the House of Girón (quartering the Royal arms of Castile and León), owners of the castle in the fifteenth century.

standing feature of Peñafiel, as in the case of earlier frontier castles, was its war-like exterior. The Arabs had been forced back from the Duero by the time the castle was built, but its construction followed the canons of earlier European military architecture, as seen in Conway Castle in Wales, with the emphasis on strong fortification. Hence the castle had a low outer wall of enceinte with the entrance through an arched gate defended by a moat. What appears to be an extension of the moat was planned along the eastern front, and traces of work on it are clearly visible. It was, however, left unfinished and exposing the foundations of the low wall of enceinte. Corbels still remain above the entrance which, although without arrow or gun-slits, was protected by machicolations. The two corbels above the door recall Conway, which, as mentioned before, seems to have inspired certain features of Peñafiel. In both castles, these corbels, that supported long vanished machicolations, are still visible today. Curiously enough, no equivalent of the massive gate at Conway was built in Spain.

Once past the first wall, the visitor finds himself in a middle ward

defended by a second, quite strong wall of enceinte with embrasures. This wall is itself reinforced by round half-towers, projecting beyond the wall, which enabled the soldiers to cover the whole area of the middle ward from their platforms.

The curtain wall at Peñafiel is impressive, with its wide wall-walks behind the merlons, following almost the entire perimeter, and the raised archery platforms on each tower. The curtain wall was not only strong but gracefully designed with alternating slender and heavy towers and decorative corbelled stonework around the battlements. Its elongated, vessel-like shape, stranded majestically on the top of a Castilian hill, makes Peñafiel one of the most remarkable structures of its time. This castle alone would be the pride of a nation.

A heavy door, protected by towers on both flanks, gives access to the inner ward. This enclosure is divided into two parts, or baileys, by a wall, with a door in the centre, and is protected by a moat and a gun-port as well as from above by corbels, indicating machicolations. The division of the enclosure and the position of the moat again recall Conway. In Peñafiel, the moat is 10 feet wide and runs across the

Peñafiel: interior of the keep; on the left is the staircase to the upper floor.

inner bailey, at that point approximately 45 feet wide. No draw-bridge mechanism remains, so it would be reasonable to assume that the moat was spanned by a single plank, easily lifted if danger threatened.

Other quite involved methods of defence were used beyond the moat and barrier. The keep itself, a massive tower 112 feet high crowned by machicolations, had a plinthed base to prevent mining and could only be entered by crossing two more removeable bridges. Its entrance was 12 feet above the ground level of the inner ward and it was covered by a gaping gun-port.

The passage giving access to the keep's hall ran inside the wall and followed a right-angle or dog's-leg course intended to prevent anyone entering the feudal Master's sanctuary without his knowledge. This type of access was a common architectural feature in the Middle Ages. A similar but less efficient design, of later date, was used in the keep of the castle of Fuensaldaña.

The two baileys housed a number of buildings for the use of servants and soldiers. They are no longer standing today; but three super-imposed chambers, reached by stone steps, are still visible at the north end of the inner bailey. The roof of the upper chamber served as a raised archery platform on this strong tower, which forms the 'prow' of the castle. The outer bailey has only two superimposed chambers at its southern extreme. The top platform can be reached by stone stairs on either side of the upper chamber.

The keep was the heart of the castle. It was built in the middle of

the fifteenth century and was, therefore, of a later date than the original castle built by Don Juan Manuel. It had a main hall with two ample windows built in alcoves in the walls which also contained comfortable stone benches. A staircase in the south-west corner led to the upper floors. Today the bare interiors are still there, with holes to show the positions of the beams which supported the upper floors. Carved on the façade is the Royal coat-of-arms of Castile and Aragón and that of the powerful House of Girón, the owners of Peñafiel during the final stages of its reconstruction. V. Lamperez has noted[3] that, considering its inhabitants' almost regal way of life and the glory of *El Conde Lucanor*[4] having been written there, ' the rooms of the strong *torre del homenaje* are mean ' while ' the defences are great and powerful '.

[3] *Arquitectura Civil Española*. Madrid, 1922.
[4] A masterpiece of imaginative prose in the form of fifty didactic tales, written by Don Juan Manuel.

La Mota, Medina del Campo: curtain wall and moat; the drawbridge is unfortunately missing from the old entrance on the right.

As previously indicated, these remarks do not allow for the fact that Don Juan Manuel inhabited a different, or lower, castle at Peñafiel. However, knowledge of this in no way diminishes the greatness of the present castle which, together with Medina del Campo and Torrelobatón, links the castles of the Reconquest and the castle-palaces of the late fifteenth century.

LA MOTA, MEDINA DEL CAMPO

The *torre del homenaje* of La Mota towers high above the town of Medina del Campo. La Mota was an important trade centre in the Middle Ages and, as such, the existence of a powerful castle to defend its eastern approach was essential.

Built of Castilian brick, La Mota is a synthesis of the successive phases of reconstruction and addition that it has undergone since at least as early as the reign of Alfonso VIII in the twelfth century. It was, however, in the fifteenth and sixteenth centuries that the castle attained its present form, after a series of alterations ordered by John II and Ferdinand and Isabella, that transformed it into a fortified palace of great strength. The trapezoidal plan included a crenellated outer wall, with circular towers and a strong gatehouse—bearing the insignia of their Catholic majesties—which housed the portcullis and a draw-bridge to span the deep moat.

The defences, which included a barbican, were begun for John II around 1440 by Fernando de Carreño, and completed by Alonso Nieto towards 1479. They had some interesting architectural features. The outer perimeter of the castle, for example, was defended not only from the wall-head, but also from two superimposed passages hollowed out of the curtain wall, which was pierced at regular intervals by loop-holes of the 'cross and orb' type for the use of fire-arms. Beyond the gatehouse and the wall of enceinte, La Mota's fortifications dated from a much earlier period, with walls of considerable height supported by square towers and enclosing the *torre del homenaje* at one corner. The walls were made partly of *mampostería* (pebbles and cement) as in the Arab *tapias*, instead of being entirely of brick. This rectangular redoubt is thought to correspond to the plan of a primitive castle built in the thirteenth century.[5] In support of this theory, the corner towers still show narrow arrow-slits for longbow use. On the other hand,

[5] Lampérez, while indicating possible Roman and Moorish traces, dates this primitive castle 'most probably' from the late Middle Ages.

La Mota, Medina del Campo: the main gate seen from the middle ward.

the justly famous *torre del homenaje* is typical of the fifteenth century, with its elegantly corbelled parapets. This tower also shows the remains of supporting arches for another storey, so it must have been extremely high, rising almost like a spire from the main body of the structure which was sunk deep in the moat. The keep and certain parts of the northern wall are attributed to Fernando de Carreño.

The castle of La Mota was meant for war. In the middle of the fifteenth century it is believed that its occupants successfully resisted a ten-month siege by noblemen who were demanding that Henry IV withdraw the privileges he had accorded to his favourite, Beltrán de la Cueva. On the other hand, there is little evidence to support the theory that it was also in this castle that the announcement was made of the marriage of Henry's unhappy daughter, Joanna *la Beltraneja*, to the Duke of Goyena, brother of Louis XI of France. The marriage, by the way, was never consummated.

The castle also served as a prison, as in the case of Joanna the Mad, daughter of Isabella of Castile, who was detained there on her mother's orders when the princess was preparing to join her husband, Philip the Handsome. On another occasion Caesar Borgia, son of Pope Alexander VI, was held in the castle, but he managed to escape with the help of the chaplain of La Mota who provided him with a file to cut open the grilled window of his cell and a rope to climb down to the bottom of the dry moat. Caesar who, according to M. J. Quintana,

La Mota, Medina del Campo: the keep

La Mota, Medina del Campo

was a kind of prodigious monster who incorporated at one and the same time ' the frenetic ferocity of Caligula, the deep and malignant astuteness of Tiberius and the brilliant and courageous ambition of Julius Caesar ', had been arrested in the castle of Castelnuovo in Naples by the order of Gonzalo Fernández de Córdoba. After his escape from La Mota, Caesar Borgia found protection in Navarre and helped its king in his struggles to defend his crown. There the son of Pope Alexander VI died in a brawl in 1507. Hernando Pizarro, brother of the conqueror of Peru, was also imprisoned at La Mota towards 1562.

The castle and town of Medina del Campo are closely connected with Isabella of Castile and have a place of unique importance in the

La Mota, Medina del Campo: corner tower seen from the middle ward, with steps leading up from the wall walk to the firing platform; below is an entrance to the passages which run inside the curtain wall.

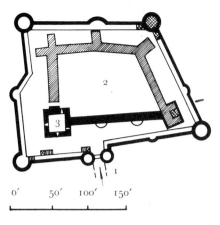

LA MOTA, MEDINA DEL CAMPO
Ground Plan
1 Masonry Bridge
2 Inner Ward
3 Keep

13th Century

Built by Fernando Carreño and
Alonso Nieto 15th Century

Outer Walls and Towers
15th Century

Modern Reconstruction

Top
*La Mota, Medina del Campo: detail of a
gun-loop of the 'cross-and-orb' type.*

*La Mota, Medina del Campo: part of the
curtain wall showing two gun-loops and an
entrance to the passages running inside the
wall.*

history of Spain. According to tradition, it was there that the great queen wrote her testament, and she was presumed to have died there in 1504. However, tradition here is not supported by fact, for it is known that Isabella died in her Palace of Medina del Campo. At all events, she appreciated the military importance of the castle of La Mota and intended to use it, because of its location and fortifications, as the Archives of her kingdom. This function was subsequently fulfilled by the castle of Simancas.

Restored in 1913 and again after the last Civil War, La Mota now houses a training school for the feminine section of the Spanish Federation of Labour (F.E.T.).

La Mota, Medina del Campo: a section of the castle showing the square towers of the older part and the newer round corner towers and outer curtain wall.

La Mota, Medina del Campo: the gate towers and bridge (a modern reconstruction) over the moat.

FUENSALDAÑA   Basic Ground Plan
(*After G. T. Clark* in Mediaeval Military Architecture in England)

1 Inner Bailey
2 Lifting Bridge

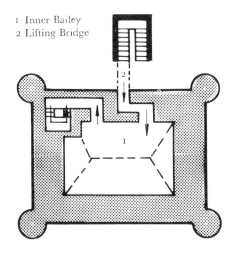

[6] *Castles of the Western World.* London, 1952.

FUENSALDAÑA

Built of finely dressed ashlar, the castle of Fuensaldaña overlooks the plains north of Valladolid. Its plan is rectangular, with round towers at the corners and a beautifully proportioned *torre del homenaje* built into the northern wall.

This castle, with its excellent crenellation work, arrow-slits and gun-ports covering all possible angles of attack, is particularly interesting in its clear application of methods of defence commonly used in the fourteenth and fifteenth centuries. Its regular plan, quite obviously associated with similar fortresses scattered throughout Castile, particularly in the Leonese region, bears out Tuulse's comparison with the Château de Vincennes in France.[6] French influence during the Reconquest was unquestionably of great importance, as will become apparent when we discuss the Spanish Military Orders. However, it is also true that a castle such as Fuensaldaña, built in the fifteenth century when the epic struggle between Christian Spain and Islam was practically at an end, fulfilled the architectural requirements of the Spanish nobility. Fuensaldaña and other similar castles of the plains had a function and importance quite different from that of the royal Château de Vincennes, built in the preceding century.

The castle of Fuensaldaña was built by Don Alfonso **Pérez** de Vivero, Chief Accountant of King John II and a member of a powerful Castilian family that played an important role in the troubled history of Spain in the fifteenth and sixteenth centuries. Don Alfonso was murdered in Burgos by order of Don Alvaro de Luna, the King's favourite, on Good Friday, 1453. But Don Alvaro did not long survive this crime, and was beheaded in Valladolid by order of his King and master on June 2 of the same year. Revenged, Don Alfonso Pérez de Vivero's tomb could boast the slightly misleading epitaph: ' *Murió por ser leal a la corona real* ' (Died for loyalty to the royal crown).

Later, a relative, Don Juan de Vivero, sponsored the wedding of Isabella of Castile to Ferdinand of Aragón. The marriage in fact took place in Vivero's house in Valladolid and this gave rise to the legend that his family's castle in Fuensaldaña was used by their Catholic majesties for their honeymoon; but no proof exists of this.

In the sixteenth century, Fuensaldaña played a significant role in the internal struggles against Charles V. The Comuneros, supporters of Joanna the Mad, took refuge in the castle during the ill-fated rebellion against the Hapsburgs, but managed to hold it only for a brief period. Years after the Crown's victory at Tordesillas, Philip II, Charles's son, granted the title of Count of Fuensaldaña to Don Juan de Vivero, Viscount of Altamira, Alcañises and Balbases.

Fuensaldaña

Although built in the fifteenth century, the castle has certain features of an earlier date. The main one is the door, a pointed Gothic arch opening off a narrow passage on to the inner ward. As in so many other examples in Spain, the castle's main entrance is adjacent to the keep and defended on one side by the keep's impressive machicolations (among the best in Spain), and on the other by the north-east tower, well furnished with gun-ports and other means of defence. Each of these corner towers has a spiral staircase leading from the *patio de armas* to the wall-head. As usual, the inner ward should have contained a number of secondary structures, such as stables, storerooms and barracks. However, with the exception of a double line of corbels projecting from the curtain wall, no traces exist of these buildings. Bordejé, in fact, maintains that the castle was never finished and doubts that it was ever permanently inhabited.[7]

A draw-bridge gave access to the keep through a door one floor above the *plaza de armas*. A passage running in the thickness of the keep's wall, following the classic dog's-leg design as at Peñafiel, leads to the low-ceilinged main room. The two upper floors are reached by a staircase in the south-east corner of the keep. Under the main room of the keep is a windowless chamber with iron rings fastened to the walls: this may have been a dungeon or *in pace*. Gamazo suggests, more prosaically, that the chamber was simply for storing weapons.[8]

Fuensaldaña: the curtain wall and two corner towers and, behind, the keep.

[7] *Castles Itinerary in Castile.* Madrid, 1965.
[8] *Castillos en Castilla.* Madrid, 1955.

Today the strong walls are still intact, but the interiors are lost, and the whole structure seems wrapped in the silence of decay. A century ago Juan Zorrilla wrote a beautiful epitaph for the proud castle:

' *De la pompa feudal, resto desnudo,*
Sin tapices, sin armas, sin alfombra;
hoy no cobija su recinto mudo
mas que silencio, soledad y sombra.

Los pájaros habitan la techumbre
y le tapiza la afanosa araña
y eso guarda la tosca pesadumbre
del viejo torreón de Fuensaldaña.'

(Naked remain of feudal pomp,
without tapestries, arms, or carpets,
today its mute enclosure shelters
only silence, loneliness and shadow.

Birds live in the vaulted roof
and busy spiders weave tapestries over it.
They guard the harsh sorrow
of the old tower of Fuensaldaña.)

SIMANCAS

On the road that leads south-west from Valladolid towards Tordesillas and Medina del Campo stands Simancas; its history goes back to Roman times, when it was known as Septimancas. Later the site of bloody encounters with the Moors who built an *alcazaba* or fortress there, Simancas, after being reconquered by the Christians, was besieged and occupied by the invincible Al-Mansur. The event is described in a contemporary document: ' [He] surrounded the fortress and, subjecting it to his bows and arrows, demolishing its walls and opening its doors, entered with ferocity . . .'[9]

The present castle, the product of frequent phases of expansion and restoration, still retains its outer defences: a moat, thick walls and crenellated towers. The stone bridges, originally of the draw-bridge type, span the moat to the east and west. Unfortunately, the main body of the fortress has been transformed, through successive attempts at restoration, into a meaningless conglomeration of styles. Juan de Herrera, one of the architects who worked here in the middle of the sixteenth century, tried unsuccessfully to preserve the austere character of Simancas, in accordance with the wishes of his patron, Philip II. It was also Philip II who, following a suggestion of Cardinal Cisneros, already approved by his father Charles V, finally housed the National Archives in Simancas, where they have remained until the present time. It seems appropriate that the historical records of Spain should be preserved within powerful stone walls whose gun-ports are still intact. Indeed, the Simancas archives are unique and invaluable, the many thousands of folios they contain testifying to the vicissitudes of a glorious past.

[9] Mentioned by Sainz de Robles in *Castillos en España*. Madrid, 1962.

Before the reign of Philip II, during the fifteenth and sixteenth centuries, Simancas, like many other Spanish castles, suffered the ignominious fate of being used as a prison. One of the towers of the wall of enceinte was, in 1521, the place of execution by *garrote vil* of the Bishop of Zamora, Don Antonio de Acuña, a captain in the Comunero forces. After the defeat of the Comuneros at the battle of Villalar, Acuña was taken prisoner and, during an effort to escape, killed one of his guards. The same Bishop Acuña was responsible for raising a battalion of 500 clergymen who, according to the chronicles, blessed their enemies with their guns before shooting them.

Earlier, the castle had held another famous prisoner: the great Master of the Order of Calatrava and Constable of Castile, Don Alvaro de Luna, who, after falling from his pedestal as King John II's favourite and adviser, was imprisoned in Simancas before being beheaded at Valladolid in 1453.

The Count of Gamazo mentions that the Simancas coat-of-arms, visible on the lintels of the fortress, was surrounded by seven hands. These unusual symbols are part of a legend: during the Arab occupation, one hundred Christian virgins were delivered yearly to the local chieftain as a tribute. One year, seven of the chosen virgins decided to cut off their right hands rather than become slaves in a Moslem harem. As a result they were incarcerated in the *alcazaba* of Simancas instead of being delivered to the Arabs. Verses from the *Gratia Dei* refer to this episode as follows:

> ' *por librarse de paganos*
> *las siete doncellas mancas*
> *se cortaron sendas manos,*
> *y las tienen los cristianos*
> *por sus armas en Simancas.*'

(to free themselves from pagans,
the seven (one-armed) virgins
cut off their hands,
which the Christians have now
as their coat-of-arms in Simancas.)

Pedraza: outer wall with gun ports.

SORIA GUADALAJARA CUENCA

These three provinces of Castile contain some of the best examples of the typically Spanish *castillos roqueros*, as well as castle-palaces of great merit and imposing ruins of Arab origin.

For centuries the province of Soria was at the frontier between the two warring faiths, and the scene of much bitter fighting. The Duero river flows through Soria on its long journey towards Portugal and the Atlantic, and the Arabs had to build their *alcazabas* overlooking its banks in order to defend their territory. Of these, none was more impressive than Gormaz, which could house hundreds of men and horses. The province of Soria was the site of the clash between the legendary Cid and the ruthless Al-Mansur over the control of Gormaz and other bastions in the area.

Guadalajara, south-west of Soria, was on the strategic road that led from Navarre (and France) towards Madrid and Toledo. It was strongly defended by castles such as Atienza, a tower rising sheer from the rock that serves as its foundation, and Sigüenza, an early Arab fortress later converted into the sumptuous castle-palace of the Archbishops of this ancient diocese.

The Tagus flows through the southern part of the province of Guadalajara. The Order of Calatrava, after the reconquest of Toledo in 1085, received extensive grants in this area, including Zorita de los Canes and Anguix. These are good examples of those fortresses that once reinforced the natural barrier of the Tagus and defended the access to the capital, Toledo. Later, they passed into the possession of noble families such as the Mendozas and Medinacelis.

Cuenca in the south-west, closely connected with the Order of Santiago, continues the outer circle of Castilian provinces. Within its boundaries are the castle-convent of Uclés, where, it is believed, the Order of Santiago established itself towards 1174, and where its Masters took possession of their titles. Also in the province of Cuenca is the important Arab fortress of Alarcón. This stronghold, on the southern approaches to Toledo, was considered impregnable, until it was conquered after a bloody siege that lasted nine months. It was granted to the Knights of Santiago in 1184.

After the period of the Reconquest, the province of Cuenca was held by men like Don Juan Pacheco, Marquis of Villena. He was responsible for the construction of Belmonte, one of the most interesting castle-palaces in Spain. Villena also owned the castle of Garcimuñoz, now an imposing ruin, which he had adapted for the use of artillery. According to Sarthou Carreres,[1] the Marquis's bombards were capable of firing eight-inch balls, possibly made of iron or hewn stone—a

[1] *Castillos de España.* Madrid, 1952.

84

remarkable feat for the fifteenth century. It is interesting to note, while on the subject of primitive firearms, that a bombard or *pierrerie* was an immobile weapon of limited range, while, by 1425, the arms carried by individual soldiers were only reasonably effective up to sixty yards. By comparison, crossbows and longbows had a much longer range: a longbow could reach a target 230 yards away, if used by an experienced archer. It was not possible to aim a firearm with any degree of accuracy until after the invention of the matchlock in 1450; even then, it was not until the sixteenth century that firearms became noticeably more efficient than other weapons.

OSMA

An ancient bridge crossing the Ucero River leads to the foot of a hill
crowned by the imposing ruins of a castle. This site, together with the
village of Burgo de Osma, on the opposite side of the river, has been
fortified since before Roman times, as the pre-Roman town of Uxama
was located in the vicinity. The famous Roman historian, Pliny,
mentioned Uxama, while Silvo Italicus attributed its construction to
an oriental people called Sarmats: '*Sarmaticos atollens Uxama muros*'.
The settlement was already important at the time of the famous siege
of Numantia by the Consul Pompey, when it, too, attempted to resist
the Consul's legions and suffered a similar fate. Rebuilt under Visigothic rule, village and castle became Church possessions, only to be
severely damaged by the Arab invaders in the eighth century. Alfonso I
of León reconquered it in 746, only to lose it again to the Infidels led
by Al-Mansur.

For centuries the war surged back and forth in the area and the
stronghold of Osma was destroyed and rebuilt on several occasions.
Gonzalo Téllez, a Castilian knight, restored it in 938, and so did
Sancho García in 1019; but the greater part of the present ruins dates

Osma: ruins of the castle.

2 Prescott mentions a potentially disastrous incident which occurred on Ferdinand's arrival at the castle. The Prince, who had travelled non-stop on his romantic journey from Saragossa, was greeted on arrival at the gate by a boulder hurtling down from the battlements, having been launched by a zealous sentry. Fortunately, Ferdinand's voice was eventually recognized and he was then joyfully received.

from the thirteenth century, when Osma belonged to the Bishop of Osma. At that time the village was protected by a long wall which was demolished by Bishop Montoya in the fifteenth century. In the same century Osma passed to the Dukes of Uceda and Frias, until Isabella of Castile, whose husband Ferdinand had spent the night at the castle on the way to their wedding at Valladolid,[2] granted it to the Marquis of Villena, Diego López Pacheco, and his wife, Juana de Luna, in 1503.

The castle was protected by a low outer wall, with crenellated towers looming high above the village and looking across the Ucero valley. Some of these weather-beaten towers are still standing, but the main body of the castle is a complete ruin. The original castle had an irregular plan and was built of ashlar stone. Only one of its towers, possibly the *torre del homenaje*, remains standing on the southern side.

An interesting tower, an *atalaya* or observation post, is visible from the castle on a hill overlooking both the borough of Osma and its castle. It is an isolated round construction of great antiquity, possibly of Saracen origin, which was part of Osma's defences. *Atalayas* were common in northern Spain, particularly in Guipúzcoa and other Basque provinces as well as in the Pyrenees. This one on the Ucero river may well have been part of an elaborate system of defence that connected the castle of Burgo de Osma with the neighbouring castles of Ucera and Gormaz.

Ruins of the atalaya *tower overlooking the Ucero River and Burgo de Osma.*

GORMAZ

'[Alfonso VI] gave him the enormous castle of Gormaz, which the Caliphs of Córdoba had built dominating the Duero . . .³

³ Menendez Pidal: *El Cid Campeador.*

The castle of Gormaz, built in the tenth century, is the most important example among the Arab fortresses built in Castile, comparing in size and strength with the best *alcazabas* in Al-Andalus. Gormaz and its village, together with the neighbouring village of San Esteban de Gormaz, are closely associated with the legendary figure of Rodrigo Diaz de Vivar, the Cid. In fact, the unknown poet who sang the glories of the Cid (or 'leader', from the Arab word *Sidi*) in the middle of the twelfth century may have been born in San Esteban de Gormaz.

Built on a hill overlooking the Duero, Gormaz played an important role in establishing the power of Islam in a frontier zone strongly disputed with the emerging kingdoms of León and Navarre. It was at Gormaz in 975 that the Christians, led by García-Fernández, were defeated by seasoned Moslem troops commanded by the famous general and poet, Galib. After this defeat, the Arabs kept precarious control of the Duero line for twenty-seven years. The castle of Gormaz passed eventually to the great and ruthless Arab leader, Al-Mansur. This daring marauder, who had so successfully conducted the sacrilegious attack on the shrine of Santiago de Compostela, met his fate in 1002 at Calatañazor, while advancing from Gormaz towards the neighbouring town of Medinaceli. Al-Mansur was defeated and killed at Calatañazor and the powerful bastion of Gormaz, which housed hundreds of soldiers and a good supply of livestock, surrendered in the same year. Christian supremacy began to assert itself on this section of the frontier, while down-river at Peñafiel the Count of Castile, Sancho García, captured and held the Duero line ten years later. Gormaz remains to this day a monument to the Arabs, while Peñafiel is by contrast, after successive reconstruction, a superb example of the European science of fortification adapted to the needs of the Spanish in the fifteenth century.

The castle of Gormaz consists of two main enclosures, of irregular plan, protected by a curtain wall more than 3,000 feet long and 30 feet high, supported by typically Arabic square towers. The main enclosure, built on a limestone rock whose scarred and pitted surface bears a distinct resemblance to a coral atoll, contained quarters for the Master and his soldiers, and the well. The second enclosure or ward was intended to house horses as well as the cattle needed to feed the troops; the entrance to it, through a graceful Arab arch, has only recently been destroyed. Two imposing towers, with the remains of crenellations, still stand today; so does the opening giving on to the path leading up from the village; and spacious cruciform openings in the walls that overlook the Duero have also been preserved. Apart from these, little of the castle remains.

Towards the end of the eleventh century, the castle of Gormaz was given to the Cid by his grateful sovereign Alfonso VI. The Cid had in the past judiciously refrained from retaliating, on the several occasions on which he had been unjustly accused, dispossessed or

The Ucero River: silhouetted on the hill behind is the ruined atalaya.

88

Gormaz

exiled by the king. As a faithful vassal, he received Gormaz towards the end of his life. This strong fortress was only one of the several castles and other possessions granted to him by the king. By then the animosity between the two stubborn warriors had subsided and Rodrigo Diaz de Vivar was the honoured conqueror of Valencia, Almenara, Murviedro and other Moorish citadels.

The poet who immortalized the Cid forty years after his death, does not forget his connections with Gormaz nor the powerful castle of Atienza towards the South:

128

The heirs of Carrion
   have left Ansarera
. . . they march without rest
   all day and all night;
on their left they leave Atienza
   that is a strong hill,
the mountains of Miedes
   fall behind them,
upon Montes claros
   they spur forward;
. . . farther on, on the right
   was San Esteban de Gormaz.[4]

[4] From *The Poem of the Cid*. Translated by W. S. Merwin, London, 1959.

It should be noted that some confusion seems to exist regarding the identity of the castle of San Esteban de Gormaz, which is quite separate from the castle of Gormaz itself. No record, however, seems to be available on San Esteban and an excellent map prepared by the *Asociación Española de Amigos de los Castillos* does not include it. It is, recorded, however, that the town was defended by two fortresses, one of them apparently destroyed.

The tiny village of Gormaz, lying below the imposing ramparts of its Moorish castle, is the subject of a well-known refrain:

'*Gormaz, Gormaz,*
mil vecinos tienes
y en siete te quedarás.'

(Gormaz, Gormaz,
you have one thousand neighbours
but only seven will remain.)

And this graceful curse has been fulfilled: from a prosperous community in the Middle Ages, Gormaz has since dwindled to a handful of houses.

ATIENZA

In the *Cantar de Myo Cid*, the famous mediaeval epic that described the heroic deeds of the Cid—written when Castilian had evolved sufficiently from its Latin origins to claim to be an independent language—Atienza was already important enough to receive mention. '*Atienza, una peña muy fuerte!*' (Atienza, a very strong rock) says the anonymous poet, and later he adds sadly: '*Atienza, las torres que moros las han!*' (Atienza, whose towers the Moors possess). Ortega y Gasset has compared Atienza with a ship navigating hesitantly between the sky and the earth. The castle is built on the crest of an enormous rock —a perfect example of the *castillo roquero*. Its walls, today largely in ruin, blend with the rock itself. An elongated vessel-like construction, inaccessible on the southern side where the proud remains of the *torre del homenaje* are still visible, Atienza is a man-made castle built on a natural one. The entrance, via a ramp, was on the northern side, where the milder gradient necessitated the removal of great chunks of rock in order to diminish the possibility of a frontal attack.

The town of Atienza already existed in Roman times, and subsequently became a Visigothic outpost. Its strategic position was appreciated by the Arabs, who converted it into an important fortress to strengthen the Duero frontier line which was already defended by Gormaz and other *alcazabas*. The stronghold fell into Christian hands when the Reconquest advanced beyond the barrier of the Duero in the reign of King Alfonso III (866–910). Its fate was in the balance for years, until finally the original castle was destroyed by Al-Mansur. After he died in 1002, following his defeat at Calatañazor, the position was recaptured by Alfonso VI.

It is difficult to ascertain the date of construction of the present castle of Atienza. We know, however, that the town was an important mediaeval centre, extremely well defended by two lines of ramparts and

by its castle. According to Layna Serrano, the castle was badly damaged during the Reconquest, but restored during Alfonso VII's reign (died 1157). This supports the theory that the castle is of twelfth-century origin. Important additions were made, however, in the fourteenth, fifteenth and sixteenth centuries.

The lay-out of Atienza is extremely simple: a wall of enceinte, low and rather weak, but still visible in parts, which enclosed an oblong area, is perched on a vast rock. Inside is the castle proper, with two square towers and a curtain wall, originally crenellated, of which little remains. Two perfectly delineated baileys can be seen: the outer one, between the walls of the castle and the external line of weak ramparts, and the inner bailey, or *patio de armas*. The outer bailey extends into a platform at its northern extreme, forming a connection between two sections of the first line of ramparts. This pentagonal area, a later addition, possibly of the sixteenth century, was intended for the use of artillery. In this respect, it resembles the artillery platform which was added at Zorita de los Canes, a stronghold of the Order of Calatrava in the same province. There is no doubt that the combined defences of the town and castle of Atienza, well equipped as they were for the use of the primitive artillery of the fifteenth century, must have presented a real challenge to would-be attackers.

The entrance to Atienza, over a ramp which led to the arched door of the castle, was defended by the northern tower. The southern tower served as the keep and was originally a two-storey structure, crowned

Atienza: the castle, an example of the castillo roquero, *stands guard over the town from which it takes its name.*

by an elegantly designed sentry post or *gariton*, typical of the fifteenth century. The theory that the castle was built in the fifteenth century is supported by details such as the window, which is set into the wall with side benches, in a style common in Castile during the reign of John II. The inner bailey is interesting for other reasons. It originally housed a certain number of buildings for the use of soldiers and servants, and contained the vital water wells, essential in case of siege.

In June 1446, the castle and town of Atienza were to prove their strength in a famous episode that was recorded in the Chronicle of King John II, ineffectual ruler of Castile in the first part of the fifteenth century. At that time, Atienza was part of the kingdom of Navarre and, during one of the many periods of war or revolt that marked John II's unfortunate reign, the town and its impregnable castle were besieged by the Castilian army, commanded by Don Alvaro de Luna; the king was also present on the battle-field. Artillery was then in its infancy, and obviously the trajectory of the early iron balls was not always accurately assessed. It transpired that the king had pitched

his tent too close to the walls of Atienza and was under direct fire from the ramparts. However, to move the royal tent back would have been considered dishonourable in the ritualistic struggles of the fifteenth century, so Don Alvaro decided to attack Atienza the following day, leaving the king behind with some reserve troops. This hasty attack was repulsed and, for more than sixty days, neither mining and countermining actions, nor the active use of artillery on both sides made any impression on the walls of Atienza. Eventually the town surrendered; but the castle held out until a truce was signed.

The Chronicle records these events in somewhat different terms: ' Upon the arrival of the King at Atienza, he ordered his royal camp to be pitched very close to the town . . having brought with him for the purpose of fighting a good supply of bombards and *truenos*[5]; and, as well, he brought many peons, cross-bowmen and lancers, and ordered them to attack the fortress strongly with his weapons, and since the fortress was very tall they could not take it, and because of this he ordered them to stop the attack on the fortress and to attack the town . . . ' Only in 1475 did the resilient stronghold pass finally to the Castilian Crown, Queen Isabella of Castile taking possession of Atienza after the battle of Toro.

The clumsy siege of Don Alvaro de Luna and King John was not the only one. Earlier, King Ferdinand II of León (died 1188), besieged Atienza in order to capture Alfonso VIII, the child who was to become King of Castile, and who was under the protection of the powerful Lara family in Atienza. Tradition has it that some horse traders smuggled the child-king safely to Avila disguised as one of them. The episode is still celebrated today: every year, on Whit Sunday, a horse parade passes through the narrow streets of the village.

Atienza, like so many other fortresses, was also a prison. In the fifteenth-century Chronicle of King Henry IV, mention is made of the fate of a rebellious prelate, Don Diego López de Madrid, who, from his stronghold of Sigüenza, had flouted the dictates of ecclesiastical discipline. Betrayed by a servant, López de Madrid was taken prisoner by the famous Cardinal Mendoza and sent to Atienza. There the prisoner died of ' *penas y azotes* ' (sorrows and whippings).

SIGUENZA

The ancient town of Sigüenza was already an important centre, called Segontia, at the time of the Roman conquest. Livy listed Segontia among the major Celtiberian strongholds of the Peninsula, together with Segovia, Uxama and Numantia. During the Roman campaigns to subjugate the primitive inhabitants of Iberia, the legions found themselves confronted by a strong resistance that culminated in the legendary siege of Numantia. There, 8,000 Celtiberians managed to inflict a serious defeat on the seasoned Roman troops commanded by the scions of great patrician families such as Metellus, Marcellus and Pompey. It was Scipio, with 60,000 troops and powerful siege weapons, who finally conquered Numantia, whose defenders had chosen to die rather than surrender. No one remained alive in the besieged stronghold after its capitulation, not even women and children. When the Romans entered, they found, ominously, a truly dead town.

[5] *Trueno* (thunder): primitive hand-gun common in Europe in the first quarter of the fifteenth century.

Segontia suffered a fate similar to Numantia. After putting up an heroic resistance to the onslaught of the Roman armies led by Metellus and Pompey, Segontia was finally subdued and razed to the ground. This eclipse, however, was temporary and by the time of the Arab invasion, eight centuries later, Segontia or Sigüenza was again recognized by the new conquerors as a strategic centre and they built there one of their *alcazabas*.

The *alcazaba* of Sigüenza changed hands several times during the bitter struggles of the Reconquest. It was wrested from the Moors probably in 1038 by Ferdinand I of Castile, but remained in Christian hands only for a brief period. Rodrigo Diaz de Vivar, the famous Cid, managed to reconquer it many years later; but not even his seasoned troops could keep control of the stronghold, which had to be abandoned yet again to the Arabs. It was only in 1124 that Bishop Bernardo de Agen finally took possession and from then on the castle became the residence of the Bishops of the diocese of Sigüenza.

Today little remains of Sigüenza's glorious past. The building has seen much fighting that has left its marks on the towers and walls; but it seems as if indifference has been its worst enemy, transforming the once sumptuous castle-palace into temporary housing for poor peasant families. With its walls corroded by time, with gaping holes where windows existed and pathetic roofs of discoloured tiles over the crenellated towers, Sigüenza is one of the saddest ruins in Castile.

Built on the site of the primitive Arab *alcazaba*, the castle-palace of Sigüenza, capable of housing 1,000 foot soldiers and 400 cavalry, was important during the fifteenth century as solid proof of the power of the Church. Its plan was trapezoidal, with the main axis running from north to south. Its walls, of tremendous thickness, enclosed a large courtyard with a deep well and large rooms opening on to it. Layna Serrano, discussing the cyclopean size of the walls, mentions that an old bishop managed to have his cell built into their thickness. The eastern façade was protected by a deep ravine, while the western façade had a shallow moat: the mild counterscarp can still be seen today. This façade was protected by three square towers, showing Arabic influence. The one at the north-west corner, with parts of its crenellation still visible, was the most important. The original door was on this façade, but it has been covered up. It is assumed that it was between two slender turrets, towards the south-west corner of the building, and that a draw-bridge spanned the moat. Another entrance was built on the northern side, at the beginning of the fourteenth century, for Bishop Simon Cisneros. Even though sadly disfigured today, the gate with its twin towers showing excellent machicolated work is still impressive. This was later complemented by a crenellated wall, built by order of the powerful Cardinal of Spain, Don Pedro González de Mendoza. The Mendoza family, of great importance in the history of the province of Guadalajara, was responsible for the creation of the great castle-palace of Real de Manzanares.

In 1468, the distinguished Cardinal Mendoza was involved in a strange ecclesiastical scandal, when he succeeded in wresting Sigüenza's palace from the hands of a rebellious prelate, Don Diego López de Madrid, who had taken possession of it in 1465. Don Diego had refused for three years to submit to ecclesiastical discipline. He was finally betrayed by a servant, and ended his days in the castle of Atienza, where he was sent as a prisoner by Cardinal Mendoza.

Towards the end of the sixteenth century the castle-palace of the Bishops of Sigüenza began to deteriorate, and the indifference of Mendoza's successors only accentuated the situation. In 1598 it became a barracks for the province's militia by order of Philip II. In 1710, during the War of the Spanish Succession, Sigüenza housed Archduke Charles of Austria, the pretender to the Spanish crown.

In 1808 and 1811, French troops occupied the castle-palace during the Napoleonic wars and were eventually expelled from it by the famous guerrilla leader, *El Empecinado* (the Stubborn). By that time very little remained of its past splendours, yet Sigüenza continued to figure in military history. In 1836 it was occupied by Carlist troops—supporters of Don Carlos, unsuccessful pretender to the Spanish crown against his cousin Doña Isabella—and in 1873 Sigüenza successfully resisted another siege, this time by a Carlist leader called Villalain.

The coat-of-arms of the Masters of Sigüenza quartered a crowned eagle, holding in its talons a human bone. This now seems almost symbolic of the fate of the once proud castle-palace.

TORIJA

This castle was carefully restored under the direction of the architect J. M. González Valcárcel, who has brought to light in an erudite article[6] important aspects of its construction. He has stressed the Italian influences affecting it, comparable to those that influenced the construction of Pioz in Guadalajara. Another castle, showing Italian influence and similar to Torija in its plan lay-out, is Barciense in the province of Toledo.

The castle of Torija, located on the main road to Madrid from the north-east, traces its origin to the early fifteenth century. However, an earlier fortress dating from the eleventh century is believed to have been built by the Knights Templar on a neighbouring hill. Protected by a ravine on its northern approach, Torija had a moat on the southern side. It was built to a square plan, with corner towers and a screen wall, traces of which show the site of a draw-bridge.

This castle dates from a period before the use of fire-arms became widespread. Its curtain wall is neither thick nor squat enough to resist artillery attack, but rather tall and slender, with few gun-ports. Later in the fifteenth century the castle's south-eastern tower was integrated with an exceptionally elegant *torre del homenaje*. This protruded from the square plan of the fortress and was similarly placed, in relation to the main body of it, as the unfinished square tower of Barciense. Torija's keep was a self-contained unit of defence, with access at second floor level and two upper storeys reached by a staircase built in the thickness of the wall. The entrance to the tower could only be reached by a removeable ladder—obviously an impractical system in peace-time. As a result, the *torre del homenaje* was not regularly inhabited. The *patio de armas*, on the other hand, shows traces of rooms on two floors having been built against the curtain walls. The corner towers were accessible through independent doors which also opened on to this courtyard.

[6] *Castillos de España* No. 56: bulletin published by the Asociación Española de Amigos de los Castillos. Madrid, 1967.

The village and castle of Torija played an important role in the internecine wars of the fifteenth century. In 1452, its master Juan de Puelles, a subject of the King of Navarre, surrendered the castle to the crown of Castile, represented by Iñigo de Mendoza, Marquis of Santillana, and the Archbishop of Toledo, Don Alonso Carrillo. The siege was memorable because of the effective use of bombards and other primitive fire-arms against the walls of the castle by Mendoza's forces. We do not know if the castle was severely damaged during the siege; but the keep, with graceful corbels and machicolations, may indicate that additions or repairs were carried out in the late fifteenth century.

Three and a half centuries later, in 1808, Torija's strategic importance was appreciated by the Napoleonic invaders, who used it as an advance post in their march on Madrid. Historians record the partial blowing up of the keep in 1811 by the previously mentioned guerrilla leader, Juan Martin the Stubborn, in order to prevent its use by the French armies led by Marshal Hugo.

In 1964, the castle of Torija, neglected for so many years, still showed the tremendous wound that sliced the keep in two in 1811.

HARO

According to the learned Don Angel Dotor, the stronghold of Haro protected the ancient village of the same name, of which Villaescusa de Haro (called originally Fuentebreñosa) was a modest neighbouring hamlet. In time, the latter grew in importance, while Haro eventually disappeared.

The castle of Haro had a rectangular plan, and may have been defended by a dry moat on the southern side. Although its weather-beaten walls are now in great need of repair, the impression of strength given by this compact military structure is in no way diminished. Haro dates from the early part of the fifteenth century, and belonged to the Knights of Santiago. The castle is therefore contemporary with the castle of Garcimuñoz and the castle-palace of Belmonte, both owned by Juan Pacheco, Marquis of Villena.

Near Garcimuñoz, and not very far from the village of Haro, Jorge Manrique, a famous nobleman and poet, met his fate. Mortally wounded while fighting the troops of King Henry IV, Manrique died at Santa Maria del Campo and was buried at the castle-monastery of Uclés, the headquarters of the Order of Santiago. It was Jorge Manrique's destiny to die on the parched plains of Cuenca—he who had dreamed of life as the flow of a river:

> ' *Nuestras vidas son los rios*
> *que van a dar en la mar*
> *que es el morir . . .* '

> (Our lives are rivers
> that flow into the sea
> which is to die . . .)

Time, the elements and the predatory habits of man have denuded the castle of Haro. Rising above a gentle slope on the plains of La Mancha, the ruin disintegrates progressively under an implacable sun.

BELMONTE

Surrounded by the parched plains of La Mancha, Belmonte, built in the middle of the fifteenth century, is one of the most original castle-palaces in Spain. Its six towers are at the extreme points of a star-shaped design enclosed by crenellated ramparts that are part of the wall defending the village of the same name. A contract of 1456, kept at Belmonte's Town Hall, states that the local people of Belmonte paid two-thirds of the total cost of this wall, which had to be 8 feet thick and 35 feet high, as well as the cost of four gates. Work began the following year and it is assumed that it included the construction of the present castle.

A most interesting example of a nobleman's residence in the troubled fifteenth century, Belmonte combined the basic need for defence and

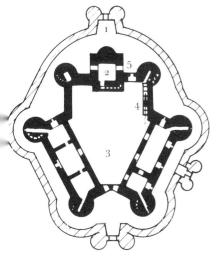

BELMONTE Ground Plan

1 Main Entrance
2 Keep
3 Inner Ward
4 Open Stairs
5 Gate

(*from* Arquitectura Civil Española *by V. Lamperez y Romea*)

security with the newly-acquired taste for luxury and comfort. Strangely enough, at a time when guns were becoming common, this castle-palace relied basically on its imposing crenellated ramparts, with old fashioned cross-bow slits and gun-loops for individual fire-arms, while no provision for heavy artillery ports seems to have been made. We know, however, that artillery and ammunition were kept inside its walls.

The main body of the castle was designed in the shape of a star with six towers at its points, enclosing a pentagonal *patio de armas*, provided with its own spring and elegant cistern. Surrounding the castle proper, a wall of enceinte, powerfully supported by crenellated towers, formed the outer defence. Its gates were protected from all angles by twin towers, while a wide platform, running behind the embrasures and merlons along the perimeter of the wall, ensured the mobility of the defenders.[7] The main gate opens today, as it did in the fifteenth century, on the opposite side to the village, which included the castle walls in its defences.

Once inside the castle's walls, the middle ward must be crossed before reaching its main entrance, protected by an imposing square keep on one side and a round tower on the other. The symmetry which is apparent in Belmonte and which reached its most perfect expression in Europe in earlier centuries (Beaumaris in Wales, Castel del Monte in Italy) still played a role in Spanish architecture in the middle of the fifteenth century. Equally important was the position of the keep, which, following the tradition of both the *roquero* castles and the castles of the plains of the fourteenth and fifteenth centuries, was located as close as possible to the main entrance. No major castle in Spain, however, reached the extreme of combining the keep with the entrance gate, a development which appeared in other European countries.

Belmonte: general view of the castle with part of the town wall visible on the left.

Right
Belmonte: the main gate.

[7] In peacetime this rampart-walk could be used as an open *loggia*.

Belmonte, with its relatively late adaptation of the general developments of military architecture, had a powerful keep. The entrance was at first-floor level, with an open staircase (i.e. vulnerable to attack from the keep) leading to it on one side of the courtyard. Once the keep's hall was reached, another staircase, running inside the wall, led to the upper chambers. Below the hall, a cell, without windows and only a trap-door from the floor above, is said to have been used for prisoners. It is still there today and can be visited quite easily, as a door has been opened through the dungeon wall from the *patio de armas*.

Two wings of the castle are obviously later additions. Their luxurious rooms form the palatial part of the structure and are exceptionally interesting because of the exuberant *Mudéjar* style employed in the interior decoration. This feature has caused Dr Lampérez to classify Belmonte among the examples of decadent Gothic architecture in Spain.[8]

The castle of Belmonte was built by the powerful Juan Pacheco, Marquis of Villena. For years it housed La Beltraneja, the unhappy daughter of Henry IV, the Impotent, after her claim to the Castilian throne was rejected in favour of Isabella's. The refuge offered by Villena was quietly transformed, for political reasons, into a golden prison. La Beltraneja, who was to end her life in a Portuguese convent without having achieved her supreme goal, believed deeply in her rights. Until her death her letters were signed with the classic ' I, the Queen ' and Belmonte was a sumptuous residence that honoured this pretension; but eventually La Beltraneja managed to escape from it, when she realized that she was being used by Villena for his own political intrigues. Tradition says that a young man helped her and that he paid for this action with his head.

[8] *Arquitectura Civil Española.* Madrid, 1922.

Colour: Sigüenza

Belmonte

La Beltraneja's spirit still pervades the rooms of this castle, superbly decorated with exquisite wooden ceilings in the best *Mudéjar* tradition and with plaster filigree of Gothic and *Mudéjar* design decorating the frames of the doors and windows. Centuries after La Beltraneja, Belmonte was again associated with a woman, a crowned queen this time: Eugenia, the Spanish wife of Napoleon III. She began long-overdue repairs, but her efforts were left unfinished after the French defeat in 1870.

Declared a national monument, Belmonte has at last been restored. Its last claim to fame is a recent one: some of the best scenes of the film, *El Cid*, were shot in its elegant courtyard in 1960.

The village of Belmonte, where the famous Fray Luis de León was born in the sixteenth century, has lost none of the bucolic character sung by the Augustinian priest and poet four centuries ago. However, little of the 'beautiful wood' which gave Belmonte its name now remains, and few green patches break the rich purple of the fields. The atmosphere of the place is beautifully expressed in the words of Fray Luis, teacher at Salamanca and friend of Saint John of the Cross, perhaps one of the purest stylists in the Spanish language. 'The air is serene and full of new beauty and light, Salinas, when that music, that supreme expression that obeys your wise hand, resounds' he wrote to his admired friend, the musician Salinas.

THE PROVINCE OF AVILA

The land of Queen Isabella, who was born in the ancient city of Madrigal de las Altas Torres, this province was also the birthplace of another remarkable woman: Saint Teresa of Avila. Hers was the purest voice of Spanish mysticism that had its masculine counterpart in the religious writings of Saint John of the Cross. The two-fold spirit—religious and war-like—of the Crusades is embodied within the ramparts of Avila. Avila of the Knights and of the Saints, as Miguel de Unamuno calls it, is indeed a castle-convent, enclosed by strong walls which protect it from the outside world: its quiet streets still ' sing our hunger of eternity '.[1] Teresa of Cepeda was born in Avila in 1515; and twenty years later this resolute but delicate woman joined the Carmelite convent of the Incarnation, so taking her first step on the road to sainthood.

Madrigal de las Altas Torres, the birthplace of Queen Isabella, was also a walled city. Unfortunately, its fortifications have not withstood the ravages of time and have partially disintegrated. Built by Moslem masons, Madrigal's walls were made of *tapia* alternating with layers of brick. Its main gate, called *Canta la piedra*, was defended by a strong, detached tower or *torre albarrana*, decorated with typical Moslem brick-work.

The western limits of the province are marked by the imposing Sierra de Gredos. There, strategically located, stands the superb Mombeltrán, while towards the south, Arenas de San Pedro overlooks the road that today still runs from Madrid to Salamanca and Portugal.

Other castles in this province are Aunqueospese in Sotalbo and Valde-Corneja near Barco de Avila. The first is of the *roquero* type and belongs to the Duke of Medinaceli; the second is more recent, dating possibly from the middle of the fifteenth century. It is of regular plan and has an enormous rectangular keep with *Mudéjar* windows. Neither structure is important historically, though Valde-Corneja, with its superb line of corbels, has architectural interest, its style being mid-way between Arenas de San Pedro and the castle-palace of Mombeltrán. Also establishing a link between two different styles are Magalia or Navas del Marqués and Arévalo, but here as we will see later, the emphasis is on the use of artillery.

Avila: the apse of the Cathedral with crenellations.

THE CITY OF AVILA

Avila occupies a privileged position in the history of military architecture, being the most impressive walled city in Europe. The ramparts, in strong granitic stone and supported by eighty-eight monumental towers, are almost two miles long. The wall encircles

[1] *Por Tierras de Portugal y de España* by Miguel de Unamuno. Colección Austral; Madrid, 1941.

the whole town of Avila, with nine heavily fortified main gates ensuring communication with the rest of Castile. Among these, the gate of San Vicente, protected by twin towers, is the most imposing and overlooks the busy traffic on the road to Madrid and Segovia.

Most historians agree today that the walls of Avila, which show strong oriental and Byzantine influences, were not originally built by Raymond of Burgundy, son-in-law of King Alfonso VI of Castile and León. His contribution seems to have been confined to reconstructing the existing fortified ramparts which had originated in Roman times. Work on the walls may have begun in 1090, but the popularly accepted theory that the designs were prepared by the Italian, Cassandro, and the French Master of Geometry, Florian de Ponthieux, is disputed. Lampérez in fact denies the mere existence of these 'Masters of Geometry'. However, it is certain that nearly 2,000 men, among them Jewish, Moslem and Christian masons, were engaged on this ambitious project.

The walls were completed in 1099, thus adding to Castile's defences

Avila: the San Vicente gate.

Avila: detail of the Cathedral door.

Avila: the city wall.

an important bastion for the war against the Moors. The whole enterprise, ordered by Alfonso VI after the reconquest of Toledo in 1085 and carried out by Raymond of Burgundy, was a political and military one. Raymond was committed not only to building the defences, but also to increasing the population of the town, decimated by constant warfare against the Infidels.

Avila was part of an architectural trend that continued to have influence for centuries in Western Europe. Aigues-Mortes in Provence and Visby on the Swedish island of Gotland are among the best preserved examples of this trend, built respectively in the twelfth and thirteenth centuries. However, the walls of Conway in Wales, begun in 1283 to enclose and protect a town with a newly granted charter, bear the closest similarity to Avila in unity of purpose and design. Conway's walls are only 1,400 yards long, but they were designed like Avila's to strengthen royal power in a newly conquered territory. Conway, however, has the great castle as its main feature, while the town walls were meant to defend the landward approaches.

In Avila there is no castle. The whole town is a bastion and the focal point is the Cathedral. This edifice blends in with the wall, because its apse is blunt and crenellated thus forming another gigantic tower. Avila's Cathedral, an exceptional example of the Spanish Romanesque style, reminds us of the time when the spiritual leadership of the Church was combined with a secular one. This dual character remained even during the fourteenth century when the town was given by the Castilian Crown to the famous Archbishop Don Alonso Carrillo. This turbulent, ambitious prelate, more inclined to warlike deeds than religious ones, was granted Avila by a royal charter of 1466. With literal disregard for the vows of celibacy, the document states that the town could be handed down to any among his children ('*para cualquier de sus hijos que el más quisiere*').

VILLAVICIOSA

On the road from Avila to Mombeltrán, about twelve miles from Avila, a muddy path leads to a sleepy village called Villaviciosa. The Master's house, its main defence, was a small, compact construction built in the fifteenth century and expanded at the beginning of the following century. Its history seems to be lost and its military deeds are unrecorded. Today pigs run around in the front yard, while the women of the village wash their linen round the communal well.

However, Federico Bordejé, who has made a study of the castle of Villaviciosa,[2] suggests that, as it was located to the south of the Iberian *castrum* of Ulaca, it may have originated as a watch-tower guarding the southern approaches of the *castrum*. Transformed later into a manor house, the tower was enlarged and provided with a wall defining a small inner ward. In the sixteenth century, the structure included the keep, crowned with elegant corbelled work, and a round tower at the south-eastern corner, which may have been built in the fifteenth century. To this was added a tower on the western side and a

[2] *Castles Itinerary in Castile.* Madrid, 1965.

wall with gun-ports, neither of which appear to have been completed. The small castle gate was strongly protected by loopholes on the western tower, thus giving the entrance a certain resemblance to the so-called L-plan of the fourteenth-century Scottish towers in which the doorway was located in the ' re-entrant angle '.[3]

[3] See *Scottish Castles: An Introduction to the Castles of Scotland* by Dr. Douglas Simpson. Edinburgh, 1959.

MOMBELTRAN

There is a stage in the evolution of military architecture when the keep or donjon disappears. This transition, when the keep, previously protected by concentric walls of enceinte, becomes one of the towers of the wall itself, took place in Scotland and Wales between 1200 and 1270. Bothwell in Scotland and more especially Flint in Wales, which was built by Edward I in 1277, are examples of this development that seems to have reached Spain at least a century later. Typical of the new concept is Mombeltrán, one of the most interesting structures in the province of Avila, built on the Sierra de Gredos, possibly in the early part of the fifteenth century.

Mombeltrán was designed as a richly furnished castle-palace. In the Castilian tradition, it is surrounded by a low wall of granite which gives an impression of great strength because of its plinthed foundation. It should be noted that, although they differ in their function and importance, Mombeltrán has one basic feature in common with the castle of Flint: the plan. Both adopted a rectangular one with four round corner towers, one of which was enlarged to serve as the keep. The outer diameter of the main tower of Mombeltrán is about 50 feet. It contained not only the apartments of the Master of the castle, but also a chapel.

Left
Villaviciosa (Avila): part of the castle with the keep in the centre.

Mombeltrán: the main gate.

Mombeltrán

The general state of repair of the castle, externally, is good, particularly the machicolations on the main body. The interiors of the towers, as well as the living quarters built of brick in the *patio de armas*, which had a gallery running round two sides of it, are lost. Yet Mombeltrán is still an impressive reminder of the power of its builder, the favourite of Henry the Impotent, Beltrán de la Cueva. He built it after receiving the duchy of Alburquerque from his master in the first part of the fifteenth century. The castle of Mombeltrán must have been a great source of pride to Don Beltrán. The loss of its interiors and of so many details representative of an epoch is extremely sad.

Don Beltrán, who was believed to have fathered the famous

Mombeltrán: one of the corner towers with false machicolations.

114

Beltraneja, daughter of Queen Joanna of Castile, spent long periods of time at Cuéllar in the province of Valladolid. The paternity of the unhappy princess is in question today, as Beltrán's claim to fame seems to be based mainly on rumours put about by the favourite himself. At all events, he certainly played an important role in the sordid affairs of the Spanish court during Henry's reign, and unquestionably had complete control over the king. Palencia makes this comment on their relationship: '*a considerar el absoluto y desenfrenado capricho de Don Beltrán, se hubiera tenido al Rey por su esclavo*'.

In retrospect, the Duke of Alburquerque appears to have been an enormously vain man: his name was already forgotten by the reign of Henry's successor, Isabella of Castile. According to Gregorio Marañón, he was 'a man of poor ethics' well suited to his position as the favourite of a psychotic king who was 'uncouth, ugly, evil smelling, misanthropic, and very carelessly dressed and booted'.[4]

Mombeltrán

[4] *Ensayo Biológico sobre Enrique IV de Castilla y su tiempo*, Espasa-Calpe; 1960.

ARENAS DE SAN PEDRO

Arenas de San Pedro: part of the keep.

Built in around the year 1400, on a square plan with round towers at the corners and square ones dividing each side of the outer walls, Arenas de San Pedro has a massive keep, where storks now build their nests; graceful *Mudéjar* windows enliven the exterior. The building now seems lost among the humble dwellings which surround it, while others block the once beautiful view from the Tiétar river.

Arenas de San Pedro is older than neighbouring Mombeltrán, and was the property of Don Ruy López Dávalos. In 1430 it was received by Don Alvaro de Luna as part of the dowry of his wife Doña Juana de Pimentel. When Don Alvaro's enemies had engineered his execution at Valladolid, his widow lived for a while at the castle of Escalona before retiring to her father's castle of Benavente, until King Henry IV forced her to move again to Arenas de San Pedro. There she spent her sad widowhood, before granting the castle to her daughter Juana de Luna, married to the second duke of the Infantado. The castle began to go to ruin in the sixteenth century, when it was first transformed into a communal jail and later used as a cemetery. Today its interiors are totally lost.

Arenas de San Pedro: a Mudéjar *window*.

Arenas de San Pedro: looking across the Tiétar River to the castle.

Arévalo: keep and main façade.

Left
Arenas de San Pedro

⁵ Popular expression recorded by the Count of Gamazo.

AREVALO

*' Quien de Castilla señor quiera ser a Arévalo y a Olmedo en favor ha de tener.'*⁵

(He who wants to be master of Castile must keep in favour with Arévalo and Olmedo.)

The town and castle of Arévalo had, in the sixteenth century, a great strategic importance, as the above quotation suggests. The castle is located on the southern banks of the Adaja River. Its main feature is the enormous *torre del homenaje*, where it is claimed, without foundation, that Isabella of Castile lived before her marriage to Ferdinand of

Aragon. It embodies, in typically Spanish fashion, the definitive transition in military architecture that took place with the change in the position of the keep. In this respect, Arévalo reminds us of Doune in Scotland, because of the aggressive stance of the Castilian castle's keep (provided with gun-ports and cannon embrasures of exceptional size) which becomes, instead of a passive core defended by walls, a vital part of the fortifications. As such, Arévalo's keep was still equipped with artillery and strongbows in the sixteenth century. Its armaments at that time included three bronze cannon, falconets and culverines. It was indeed a stronghold, with ample *meurtrières* to defend it from the top of the battlements, even if after considerable restoration its elegant walls of white limestone, topped by brick crenellations, gave it the refined character of a Renaissance palace. The tower, four storeys high and with vaulted rooms, originally defended the sixteenth-century gate near it. The present door is the result of later restorations.

Arévalo, like so many other Castilian castles, was an important pawn in the struggles connected with the succession of Henry the Impotent. In 1445 it underwent a famous siege, when Henry attacked the rebellious nobles supporting the young Infante Alfonso, brother of Isabella. Later, the king gave the castle with its Dukedom to Don Alvaro de Zuñiga, Count of Plasencia. Today, Arévalo has been restored and is used for grain storage.

Among its interesting architectural features are the *meurtrières* mentioned earlier. These downward sloping openings in the curtain wall could be used to throw boiling water or pitch on to foolhardy attackers. This type of defence was not always found in Spanish fortified structures. In Arévalo it reminds us of similar features in Northern European fortified manor-houses, such as Gisselfeld, built in Denmark towards 1547.

Las Navas del Marqués: the main door.

Arévalo

LAS NAVAS DEL MARQUES

Mention has already been made of the famous siege of Torija in 1452, when bombards and other forms of artillery were used to demolish the defences of the castle. The increased use of these weapons naturally affected the design of castle-palaces, which were from then on conceived as relatively low, compact structures, with solid walls able to withstand the impact of cannon-balls. The use of artillery for defence, too, further influenced architecture: some castle-palaces fall into the transitional category, because they are mid-way between the fortified residence of a nobleman and the purely military fortress of the late sixteenth century.

Las Navas del Marqués, or Magalia, is a typical example of a transitional castle, and was built during the reigns of Charles V and Philip II (in spite of their prohibition of castellating or building castles). It has a rectangular lay-out with massive towers at the corners. One of these towers, on the northern side, is very large and totally disproportionate to the rest of the building; it was obviously designed as its main bulwark and, as in Arévalo (Segovia), possibly housed some pieces of artillery. Its massive walls, possibly of an earlier date than the rest of the castle, are twelve feet thick.

It was Charles V's accountant, Don Pedro Dávila, first Marquis of Las Navas, who built Las Navas del Marqués in the sixteenth century. The influence of the architect Juan de Herrera, one of the creators of the famous Escorial, is apparent in the design of this solid structure. In particular, the classical main door and the central courtyard with its galleries, are considered typical of Herrera's sober and well-proportioned style.

Las Navas del Marqués

THE PROVINCE OF SEGOVIA

This province is the true land of castles: Castilnovo, Coca, Cuéllar, Pedraza, Sepúlveda, Turégano, and the most important of them all, the Alcázar of Segovia. These fortresses, transformed eventually into palaces, played an important part in the history of Spain not only during the Reconquest, but also during the subsequent struggles over the unification of the realm. Some of these castles are unique, such as Coca, an extraordinary structure of reddish brick which is a perfect example of Gothic influence on *Mudéjar* architecture and decoration. The visual impact of its many crenellated towers and extrusions tend to make one overlook the fundamental strength of the castle's design, with immensely thick walls and numerous gun-loops and *meurtrières*. This war-like exterior, probably designed mostly for effect, has remained untried through the centuries.

Among those castles which are now in total ruin, Sepúlveda deserves a special mention. It was originally a Roman stronghold or *castrum*, and Count Fernán Gonzáles later built a fortress that owed much to Arab influence on the same site. At the height of its splendour, from the thirteenth to fifteenth centuries, Sepúlveda had important Masters, such as Don Alvaro de Luna and Juan Pacheco, the Marquis of Villena. Located at the cross-roads of religious fanaticism, Sepúlveda bore its share of the effects of intolerance and bigotry. In 1468 sixteen Jews were executed there by hanging and burning after ' secret accusations '. With the passing of time, Sepúlveda decayed. Its desperate resistance to the French invaders in 1808 contributed greatly to this process of deterioration. Today the castle is only a cluster of ruins, bearing Gothic coats-of-arms.

The respect and veneration shown for the Alcázar of Segovia is unequalled anywhere in Spain. This traditional monument, identified with the kings of Castile, was already famous in the time of Alfonso the Learned. Later, other kings made various additions. John II added the powerful tower that carries his name. Henry the Impotent lavished great care on the decoration of the fortress and no matter what critics may say about his character, they all agree that his improvements were superb. In the *Sala de los Reyes*, he placed the imposing row of seated statues of the thirty-four kings of Castile that originated with Pelayo. The statues were made of plaster covered with gilt and polychrome and, so perfect was the result, that a fifteenth-century visitor, the German Baron of Rosminthal, reported that they were made of pure gold. Other works of art included courtyards with floors of alabaster and richly decorated rooms, also reported by Rosminthal, all of which were lost in the fire of 1862, which left only the outer walls and towers standing.

Alcázar of Segovia

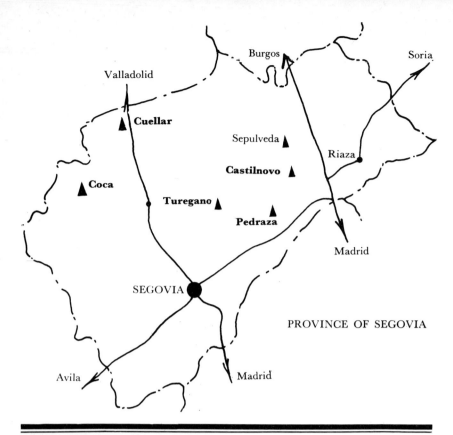

PROVINCE OF SEGOVIA

TURÉGANO

Reliable historians, such as Lampérez, have confused the castle of Turégano with the church and village of the same name. No mention is made of the castle in the thirteenth-century charter that grants the town of Turégano to the bishops of the Segovian diocese. Even when the town had the privilege, in 1399, of creating a military garrison of ninety *ballesteros* (soldiers armed with a *ballesta* or cross-bow) there is no mention of a castle. Much later, during the reign of Henry IV, mention is made of the castle of Turégano. At that time, 1466, the Bishop of Segovia is recorded as having started its construction with ' great numbers and expense ', using as the first line of defence an older wall that crowned the hill overlooking the town of Turégano. Parts of these ancient buildings are still visible today, corroded by time and the elements.

Turégano, which originated as a church and was fortified much later, runs contrary to the trend of other military-religious buildings in Spain. It is, therefore, quite different in character from those castle-palaces built by bishops as quasi-royal residences, such as Sigüenza and Coca, and also from those castles occupied by the Military Orders.

Turégano's defences were built for political purposes. They were the work of Don Juan Arias Dávila, powerful Bishop of Segovia and declared enemy of King Henry IV, during the struggle for supremacy between the Church and the Crown in the middle of the fifteenth century. Castile during the Middle Ages needed a strong, even brutal king. Henry the Impotent was certainly not the type of man required. Benevolent historians mention that his main attributes were humility, meekness and forgiveness, all of them praiseworthy, but unfortunately his subjects needed a king capable of facing the problems of the age. As a result, the unfortunate monarch who:

> ' *Por dar a muchos reposo*
> *Dio a sí gran sobresalto* '
>
> (Because he gave repose to many
> gave great agitation to himself)

was constantly harassed by the animosity of the Church, as represented by Bishop Carrillo of Toledo and Juan Arias Dávila of Segovia. The city of Segovia itself, preferred by Henry to all others, was on one occasion invaded by rebellious troops who threatened to depose the King. Although peace was restored, the Bishop of Segovia, fearing the King's reaction, left his bishopric and took refuge in Turégano, where he completed the fortifications of the castle whose construction he had begun two years before, in 1466.

With the death of the King in 1474, Don Juan Arias Dávila returned to Segovia. There he received, with great pomp and ceremony, Henry's sister, Isabella, who was proclaimed Queen of Castile at the Alcázar. In the meantime, her husband, Ferdinand of Aragón, was requested to stay at Turégano where he received the news of his wife's coronation.

All the preceding information is given by Eugenio Colorado y Laca in his learned description of the origins of the castle.[1] Its history, however, did not end with its founder. Philip II, for instance, imprisoned his secretary Antonio Perez in a dungeon at Turégano that can still be visited today. Eventually the castle passed to the Crown by a royal decree of Charles III, thus reversing its original function as an anti-royal stronghold.

The church enclosed within the castle walls is considerably older than the castle itself and is an example of the Romanesque style prevalent in Spanish religious buildings during the twelfth century. It occupies the *plaza de armas* or inner ward and contributes to the impression of mixed style and function within the massive ensemble.

The castle had a double wall of enceinte, built at different periods. Little remains of the outer wall, which is possibly of Moorish origin, but the crenellated inner one is still impressive, with powerful towers standing at the corners. Inside these walls is the castle, built by the Bishop of Segovia on a rectangular plan surrounding the church. Its walls are high and supported by round towers, with crenellations and gun-loops for defence. Three of these towers, facing west, are remarkably well preserved in their slender elegance. A wide platform allowed the soldiers easy access to their positions on the perimeter and to the raised firing stations in the towers. Turégano was indeed meant as an instrument of war.

Federico Bordejé has mentioned certain interesting similarities between Turégano and Chastel Blanc in Safita, Palestine.[2] The latter, which also had a small Romanesque church as its nucleus, was built by the Knights Templar, so this respected authority considers that Turégano may have been associated with the same Military Order. However, nothing seems to confirm this belief, since Turégano was first a church, and its fortifications were later additions. The religious building, therefore, is different in character from the chapel included in the Crusaders' castles.

[1] *Estudios Segovianos*, Vol. VIII; 1956.
[2] *Castles Itinerary in Castile*. Madrid, 1965.

COCA

The castle-palace of Coca was built in the fifteenth century by the Archbishop of Seville, Alfonso de Fonseca.

The Count of Gamazo[3] refers to Don Elias Tormo's opinion that Coca and its castle were politically connected, because of their strategic location, to the walled city of Olmedo and to the powerful castle of Arévalo. These latter strongholds were of vital importance in the fifteenth century and, according to Tormo, they constituted, together

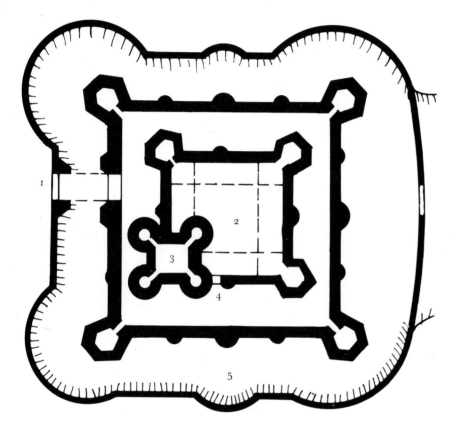

COCA

1 Entrance over bridge
2 Courtyard
3 Keep
4 Main door
5 Moat

with Cuéllar and Coca, the four points of a quadrangular area that was the key-point of the civil strife in Castile during that century.

Olmedo, due to its position between Segovia and Medina del Campo, was involved in the confused politics of John II and Henry IV. Arévalo was closely connected with Queen Isabella, who spent a considerable amount of time there. Coca and its neighbour Cuéllar, on the other hand, remained implacable enemies during her struggle for the throne.

The castle of Coca is considered the best example of the Arab influenced style of architecture and geometrical type of decoration called *Mudéjar*. The *Mudéjares* were Moslems who were allowed to live and work in the newly reconquered areas. From the early part of the fourteenth century, when King Peter the Cruel built the magnificent Alcázar of Seville, until the end of the fifteenth century, it became customary to employ Moslem labourers and craftsmen in many of the great churches and palaces of the time. Their influence blended with

[3] *Castillos en Castilla*. Madrid, 1955.

128

the art of the Christians to create a truly vernacular style. The castle-palace of Coca remains to this day the best example of *Mudéjar* work in the military field. Contrasting with the severe Castilian fortresses of stone, Coca was built with bricks that gave it a striking reddish effect. The wealth and variety of decorative designs was exceptional. From the corner towers with massive plinths to the elaborate crenellation work, Coca remains unique, not only in Spain, but in the whole tradition of European castellated structures. It is unfortunate that a building of such character does not have the natural background it deserves.

Coca was also the definitive example of symmetrical construction in Castile. It had a rectangular plan, with two major lines of crenellated walls. The first wall, ten feet thick, had massive hexagonal towers at the four corners and each façade of the towers had, in turn, a hexagonal extrusion called an *escaragüaita*. This typically Spanish form of bartizan turret appears on the keep of Peñafiel and was a basic feature of other Castilian keeps such as those of La Mota and Fuensaldaña. The massive screen wall at Coca had a tower in its centre and round bartizan turrets at each side.

Facing the bridge across the moat and protecting it were two hexagonal towers, well-provided with gun-loops of the cruciform and inverted key-hole types. The twin towers were joined by a set of projecting corbels that supported excellent machicolation work, intended apparently for defending from above the massive arch that gave access to the castle. It should be mentioned here that the moat was possibly dry and not intended to be flooded, since a number of gun-ports were placed about three feet from the bottom. Coca was built when artillery was in general use, so it was provided with a number of square openings for heavy cannon.

In spite of the apparent strength of these defences, it is difficult to think of them as more than decorative features designed more for effect than for action. This impression is reinforced when one passes the wall of enceinte and enters the middle ward. Here the walls were made partially of rubble which was contained by a narrow strip of brickwork to give an impression of solidity. The second line of walls more or less followed the basically symmetrical design of the outer ramparts. The massive *torre del homenaje* on the north-east corner was also symmetrical, with round instead of hexagonal corner-towers and *escaragüaitas*.

Both walls and towers were topped by crenellations of dark red brick, while the walls had alternate layers of different shades of lighter red brick, giving a unique decorative effect. Centuries of exposure to the elements has worn the bricks of Coca into fascinating shapes which add a fairy-tale quality to the castle. To impede further decay, the Spanish authorities began renovations in 1953. Work was completed twelve years later, and included faithful restoration of the parade ground and of rooms and galleries. Unfortunately, nothing remains of the original interiors. As Ortiz Echagüe says: 'Although its walls miraculously survived the wars since the fifteenth century the interiors were not so fortunate. They were brutally destroyed by the administration of the House of Alba which, in 1828, sold the columns and tiles of its luxurious patio.' This courtyard or patio was once famous, with its double Corinthian colonnade and its floors and walls covered with ceramics of Moorish design. Access to the inner ward was through an elegant *Mudéjar* door with a pointed arch.

This bastion was seldom touched by history and apparently was

Left
Pedraza: the old nail-studded door.

Pedraza: view from the village road of the ruins of the palatial part of the castle.

never completed. It belonged to the Fonsecas, a family descended from Don Alfonso, Archbishop of Seville, a tremendously rich cleric of the fifteenth century, 'more inclined to fighting and to courtly intrigues than to exercising austerity or setting pious examples'.[4]

At present the castle houses an Agricultural and Forestry Training College. The students cross the moat on a masonry bridge that leads to the main gate, or use the postern gate. During their free hours they can be seen strolling around the middle ward or walking on the raised platform behind the merlons and embrasures of the wall.

Some of the gun-loops at Coca deserve comment: they are in the form of 'long slits with a short crosslet slit near the top and a circular aperture at the bottom', thus being identical, for example, to those described by S. H. Cruden at the castle of Tillycairn, Aberdeenshire, Scotland. The openings were designed for hand guns and possibly arquebuses. This 'modern' weapon had its long barrel supported by a kind of crutch and was awkward and slow to load and fire. Cruden, comparing its efficiency with that of the crossbow, states that the arquebus discharged one-ounce balls at the rate of six or seven an hour, while a crossbow could fire two to three bolts a minute. Even the old longbow was more effective and precise, shooting five or six arrows a minute.

[4] Don Elias Tormo.

PEDRAZA

Spain has some excellent examples of military architecture showing its adaptability to the available site: the castle of Pedraza is one of the best of these. Built at the summit of a steep hill, Pedraza defends the small fortified village of the same name, in the heart of the province of Segovia and not far (about fifteen miles) from the town of Segovia itself.

Pedraza belonged for centuries to the House of Velazco. It had a polygonal plan and its gate on the western façade, protected by huge *escaragüaitas* or bartizan turrets on each side, shows Gothic influence. The door, covered with pointed studs, is crowned by the coat-of-arms of the fourth *condestable* of Velazco, Don Pedro Fernández, Duke of Frías, who restored the castle in 1561 and gave it the character of a palace, without destroying its formidable defences.

Pedraza: a bartizan turret in the outer wall; behind is the keep.

The castle-palace can only be reached from the village. The moat is spanned nowadays by a masonry bridge, but there was possibly once a draw-bridge. Inside the first wall of defence is the castle proper, with a square keep built of stone rubble (obviously earlier than the outer defences), and a Gothic gate with a portcullis. A remarkable line of corbels, reminiscent of Craigmillar in Scotland, adorns the eastern façade of the structure. Inside the castle is a large open area surrounded by high walls with empty Gothic windows—all that now survives of the residential section of Pedraza.

The outer wall presents a formidable array of gun openings. Some of them are a variation on the traditional gun-loop, being narrow slits with a rectangular opening at the bottom. Others, like funnels opening outwards, were intended for heavier guns. These large square openings are on a single level, except on one tower where a double row protects the bridge.

For several months after the battle of Pavia, Pedraza housed the sons of Francis I—the future Henry II, and Francis, Duke of Angoulême— who were taken as hostages to hold their father to the Treaty of Madrid which he had signed in 1526. But this is not Pedraza's only claim to fame, since the quiet village is considered by the Segovian historian, Colmenares, to have been the birthplace of the Roman Emperor Trajan. One of the last occupants of the castle was the famous painter, Zuloaga. He added the present roof to the keep which he used as his living quarters.

Pedraza: the outer line of defence and moat; the masonry bridge is modern.

Left

Pedraza: the gate-house. Above the old door is the coat-of-arms of Don Pedro Fernández, Duke of Frías.

Cuéllar: a section of the corbelled outer wall and turret.

CUELLAR

Although the strong towers of Cuéllar give it a military air, it is fundamentally a palace. A lovely gallery, supported by elaborate corbels and balconies on the southern façade, point to the transition from mediaeval spareness to Renaissance opulence.

Closely connected with the most turbulent period in the history of Castile, Cuéllar was offered by Henry the Impotent, the despised king of a divided realm, to Don Beltrán de la Cueva, Duke of Alburquerque, his favourite and adviser. No historian today would give a categorical answer to the question of whether Henry's nickname was justified or not, but his contemporaries seemed to think so. It was therefore natural that, when Henry's second wife, Queen Joanna of Portugal, gave birth to a daughter, the malicious court and later the populace should assume that Beltrán and not the King was the child's father. This unhappy girl, Joanna of Castile, went down in history as La Beltraneja. Her claim to the Castilian crown was rejected in favour of that of her cousin Isabella, crowned with the cynical approval of the arrogant nobles who even went so far as to throw the insult of Joanna's doubtful paternity in the King's face. History has proved the choice of Isabella to be the right one, as it was she who, with her royal

husband Ferdinand of Aragón, opened the glorious period of the Reconquest that was to end at Granada in 1492.

Cuéllar was the stronghold of Isabella's enemies before her accession to the throne. While the neighbouring Coca was firmly held by traditional friends, Cuéllar, a favourite residence of the Duke of Alburquerque, was consistently hostile to her. With the growing power of the Crown, Cuéllar, after playing a minor part in the War of the Comuneros in the sixteenth century, settled down to an uneventful life. The last historic occasion was in 1808 when Wellington lived there for six days during his campaign with the Spaniards against the Napoleonic invaders.

The castle forms part of the wall that surrounded the town of Cuéllar. The plan is trapezoidal, with three wings containing the palace apartments, and a crenellated wall protecting the shortest side. Excellent machicolated work and gun-ports are clearly visible. The interior included the *patio de armas* with a superb double gallery (replacing an earlier one in Gothic style) built by the third Duke of Alburquerque in 1558. In the main round tower was the chapel with a Gothic vault, and below it the original rooms, still there today: an impressive and spacious kitchen and dungeons.

While in the hands of the House of Alcañiz, Cuéllar housed a rich collection of armour and mediaeval weapons which was pillaged by French troops during the War of the Spanish Succession in the eighteenth century. Very little now remains of another great treasure— the original Plateresque work that enlivened the palace with painted beams and stucco ceilings after its restoration in the sixteenth century.

After the last Civil War, Cuéllar was used as a prison, but this unfortunate phase ended in 1965.

Cuéllar: the gallery.

Cuéllar: the round tower and gallery with decorative corbelling.

CASTILNOVO

Castilnovo, a castle-palace of rectangular plan, with six towers showing Arabic influence, has been restored on several occasions since its original construction, attributed to a minor *taifa* king. This frontier potentate had his capital at Sepúlveda, where the ruins of an imposing castle built on the site of his *alcazaba* can be seen today.

During the reign of John II, Castilnovo belonged to his omnipotent and unlucky favourite, Don Alvaro de Luna, who enlarged it. Later their Catholic majesties, Ferdinand and Isabella, were based here during some of their trips from Segovia to Burgos. Eventually, it became the property of the Galofre family, who transformed it into a sumptuous palace.

Built in a curious mixture of brick and *mamposteria*, crenellated in parts and with a graceful gallery typical of Castilian castle-palaces, Castilnovo has been kept in an excellent state of preservation and is still inhabited by its present owner, the Marquis of Quintanar. Together with Guadamur and San Martin de Valdeiglesias, Castilnovo is an example of tasteful restoration.

ALCAZAR OF SEGOVIA

The city of Segovia, important from early Roman times, is an outstanding example of a Castilian walled city. After its reconquest in the eleventh century, successive kings of Castile, including Ferdinand III, Alfonso VIII,[5] and particularly Alfonso X, extended and modified a fortified enclosure at one end of the city on a rock overlooking the confluence of two rivers, the Adaja and the Eresma. In the thirteenth century, Alfonso X made this primitive castle the favourite residence of the Castilian royalty. However, it was John II who, in the first half of the fifteenth century, gave the Alcázar the external character that it has retained until this day. John II detached the keep of the old castle, which was left as part of the new structure, and proceeded to erect a new tower, perfectly proportioned in its massive elegance. This tower, aptly called John II's Tower, is crowned by twelve half-cylinders decorated with flat, round forms and remains the most impressive and original in Castile.[6] It faced the town across the moat and was designed to match in height the steeple of the former Cathedral of Segovia. During the War of the Comunidades this steeple was—according to Don Federico Bordejé—destroyed by fire from John II's Tower.

The Alcázar of Segovia was the scene of several meetings of the Spanish Cortes. At one of these in 1383, King John I established the Christian calendar beginning with the birth of Christ, to replace the old calendar used since the time of Caesar. Traditionally it was here that Alfonso X, the Learned, expressed the theory that ' the sun did not move around the earth ', and that lightning subsequently hit the building as a sign of divine condemnation of this ' heresy '.

On the death of Henry IV in 1474, the Alcázar was the home of his sister Isabella and later it was the scene of her coronation as Queen of Castile, amid great celebrations enjoyed by thousands of Segovians. The castle was also visited by Christopher Columbus, when he came to seek audience with their Catholic majesties before leaving on the

[5] According to the Marquis of Lozoya, the old keep dates from the period of Alfonso VIII's reconstruction. This work was heavily influenced by Cistercian concepts from France. To this period belong some windows of late Romanesque style which were part of the present *Alcázar*, as discovered after the fire of 1862.

[6] The Count of Gamazo believes that John II's Tower was the inspiration, a century later, for the superb *torre del homenaje* of Belmonte de Campos, a castle-palace in the province of Palencia.

voyage which culminated in his discovery of America. In 1570 the Alcázar saw the wedding of Philip II to Anne of Austria. Philip was extremely interested in restoring the Alcázar, as he had others like Simancas and the Alcázar of Toledo. However, the Moorish influence was almost entirely lost during his restoration and was replaced by a severe, ascetic style, probably that of the King's favourite architect, Juan de Herrera. It is possible that Herrera himself did not work on the Alcázar, and that another of Philip II's architects, Francisco de Mora, remodelled the main courtyard. The turrets with pointed slate roofs and the outer battlements on the north point originated during Philip II's reign, and it was from one of the restored rooms of the Alcázar that he issued his fateful decree on the expulsion of the Moors from Spain.

In the middle of the eighteenth century, the castle became the Royal College of Artillery and continued in this capacity until it was gutted in the fire of 1862. Photography was already flourishing in the 1860s and we have numerous pictures of the Alcázar of Segovia before and after the fire. It is apparent from these that most of its pointed roofs were destroyed, while John II's Tower remained almost unscathed. The rest of the structure was reduced to a pathetic shell, with gaping holes where the windows had been. A glassed-in gallery running along the main façade, a relatively modern addition in dubious taste, was particularly vulnerable to the flames and it was not reconstructed when restoration work began in the 1880s. Another addition which was not replaced was a clock on John II's Tower.

The reconstruction, completed in 1890, preserved the slightly Germanic flavour of the Alcázar, reminiscent of the Black Forest and its fairy-tale castles. This foreign touch, however, in no way detracts from the majesty of a building which has no parallel in Spain.

Alcázar of Segovia: towers and slate roofs in the Bavarian tradition.

This page
Alcázar of Segovia: John II's Tower, with the then Royal coat-of-arms—the arms of León and Castile combined—on the battlements.

THE PROVINCE OF MADRID

The city of Madrid only became the capital of Spain in 1561, when Philip II transferred his court there from Toledo. The town, known as Magerit by the Arabs, did not have a Mediaeval castle, but its *alcázar*, gone today, was a famous example of early Renaissance influence in Spain.

Within the province of Madrid, two castles of different origin are well known: the ancient Arab fortress of Buitrago and the castle-palace of Real de Manzanares. Others, such as the well restored San Martin de Valdeiglesias or the mutilated Chinchón, built in the fifteenth century, deserve notice. But also some smaller ones, such as Villarejo de Salvanés, Pinto and Torrejón de Velazco, are of particular interest because of the restrained use of cubic, cylindrical and other geometrical shapes in their basically functional design.

Villarejo de Salvanés, with a tall round tower as its only extant building, is possibly the most interesting. The fortress belonged to Don Luis de Requesens, who fought with Don Juan of Austria in the battle of Lepanto. The neighbouring village still houses the painting

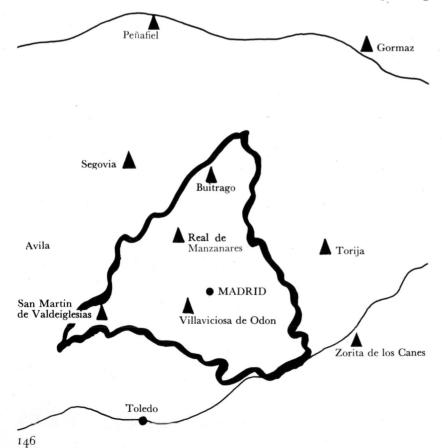

El Real de Manzanares: the gallery on the southern façade in the style called Isabelino.

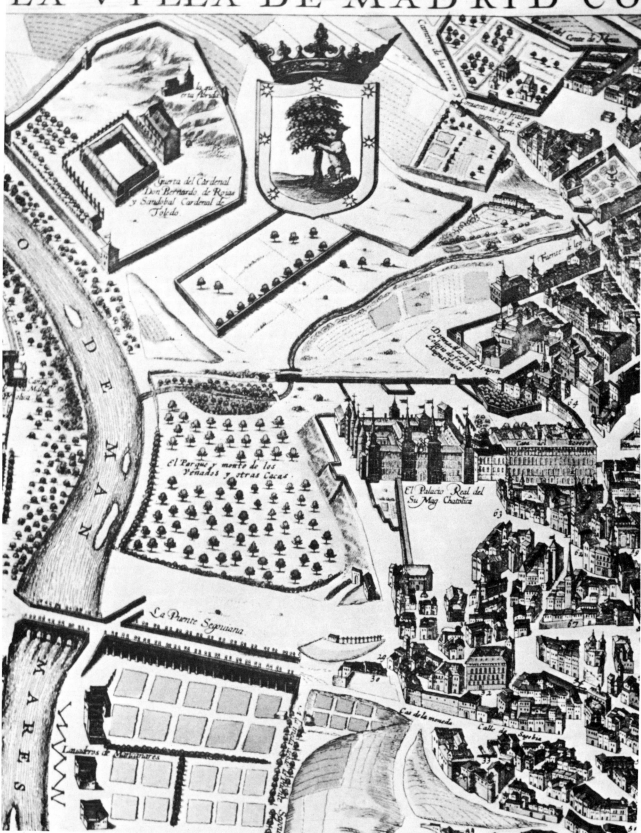

of the Virgin of Our Lady of Lepanto given by Pope Pious V after the great victory against the Turks. Pinto, another fortified tower, is famous for a different reason. In 1579, the princess of Eboli, mother of the first duke of Pastrana, was detained there by royal decree of Philip II.

Among the walled cities in the province of Madrid, Alcalá de Henares achieved importance in the sixteenth century as a major centre of learning. Its University, associated for ever with Cervantes, and its famous palace of the Bishops, have maintained their prestige through the centuries. Alcalá was the fief of turbulent prelates such as the famous Carrillo, as well as of the enlightened Cardinal Cisneros, who founded the University in 1508.

ALCAZAR OF MADRID

' Reinando Ramiro II seguro (en León) consultó con los magnates de su reino de que modo invadiría la tierra de los caldeos y juntando su ejército se encaminó a la ciudad que llamaban Magerit, desmanteló sus muros, hizo muchos estragos en un domingo, y, ayudado de la clemencia de Dios, volvió a su reino en paz con su victoria.' [1]

(During Ramiro II's reign, secure [on the throne of León], the King consulted with the dignitaries of his realm on the best way to invade the land of the Infidels and, gathering his army, marched to the city they called Magerit, tearing down its walls, causing great losses during one Sunday, and, helped by God's clemency, returned to his Kingdom in peace with his victory.)

The ancient site of present-day Madrid was already an important Moslem outpost in the tenth century: it is thought that Al-Mansur used it as a base for some of his forays against the Christian kingdoms of Castile and León. The position was conquered towards 1083 by Alfonso VI and thereafter resisted the attacks of the Almorávides and Almohades. The original Arab fortress eventually became a royal *alcázar* which underwent considerable restoration under the kings of the House of Trastamara, particularly Henry III. Later, under Charles V, the great Alcázar reached the height of its splendour and could compare with those of Segovia and Toledo. According to seventeenth-century drawings, the Alcázar was an imposing structure, in severe Renaissance style, standing on the steep banks of the Manzanares River.

The castle-palace witnessed many important events, such as the luxurious wedding of Henry IV and Joanna of Portugal. Here, too, Joanna was later kept prisoner when she was accused of illicit relations with the court's favourite, Don Beltrán de la Cueva.

In 1474, Henry IV died at the Alcázar of Madrid. When the unhappy king felt the approach of death he tried to escape on horseback to the then wild country around El Pardo. But he had to give up his attempt, and, returning to Madrid he went to bed fully clothed and so died in the morning of December 12 at 50 years of age. ' The funeral was miserable and abject. The corpse, placed on old planks, was taken without any pomp, on the shoulders of people hired for the

[1] *Chronicle of the Silos monk*, c.1080, mentioned by Sainz de Robles in *Castillos en España*. Madrid, 1962.

occasion, to the monastery of Santa Maria de Paso.'[2]

When Madrid became the capital of the Spanish monarchy in 1561, its Alcázar was the centre of events affecting the most powerful empire of the time. For almost two centuries the building was the residence of Spanish kings, until a fire destroyed it utterly on Christmas Eve of 1734. Nothing remains of the Alcázar today. Its primitive architectural style was replaced by current French influence when Philip V of Bourbon built the present royal palace on its foundations.

BUITRAGO

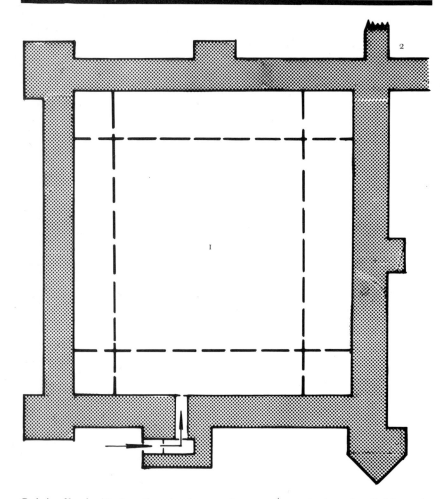

BUITRAGO   Basic Ground Plan
(*from* Arquitectura Civil Española *by V. Lamperez y Romea*)

1   Inner Ward
2   Town Walls

Originally built by the Arabs as the northern bulwark of Magerit (Madrid) on the Guadarrama hills, the present castle of Buitrago dates from the fourteenth century. It is reputed to have housed Henry of Trastamara in 1368 and to have played a part in his war with Peter the Cruel.

Buitrago is a classic example of the *Mudéjar* style of brick construction. Unlike the castle of Coca, which was also built of brick, Buitrago has an austere appearance with some external decoration, as for instance the windows in the Moslem pointed arch style. It is believed that the castle-palace had superb wooden ceilings, but no trace of them remains today.

[2] *Ensayo Biológico sobre Enrique IV de Castilla y su tiempo* by Gregorio Marañón. Espasa-Calpe; 1960.

Buitrago: rectangular corner tower with a window showing Arabic influence.

Buitrago was the strongest bastion of the House of Mendoza. It was a powerful structure on a square plan with typical Moorish square towers, one of them incorporating a wedge-shaped design introduced by the Arabs which also occurs in the castles of Montalbán (Toledo) and Montealegre (Valladolid). Access to it was protected by a barbican which followed the right-angle design common to many Castilian fortresses. The structure included a *patio de armas* or courtyard, with rooms on two storeys opening on to it. Here at Buitrago the famous Iñigo López de Mendoza, Marquis of Santillana, entertained King John II of Castile in 1435. It was here also that La Beltraneja was detained in the custody of Mendoza in 1467, when her mother, Queen Joanna, in connivance with the feudal lord, came to see her.

This proud castle-palace, representing the great power of the Castilian nobility, was still imposing in the eighteenth century. Unfortunately, it was partially destroyed by retreating French troops during the War of Independence at the beginning of the nineteenth century.

Today Buitrago, built on the banks of the Lozoya River, is a complete ruin. The walls of the castle once merged with those of the ancient town of Buitrago; today houses are built outside those ancient walls, but traces of Arab domination and influence are still visible, particularly in the gate leading from the church square to the new neighbourhood.

Buitrago: classical Moorish-style gateway.

EL REAL DE MANZANARES

Colour: Anguix

King John II gave the *señorio* of Manzanares to the first Marquis of
Santillana, Don Iñigo López de Mendoza, a distinguished soldier and
politician, who was also one of the most important writers in Spain
in the fifteenth century. This territory, on the southern slopes of the
Guadarrama hills, was contested for centuries between the cities of
Segovia and Madrid. It originally had a castle, built in the thirteenth
century by Segovian forces, of rectangular plan with round towers on
three corners and a larger square one which served as the *torre del
homenaje* on the fourth. The present castle of Real de Manzanares was
confused until recently by historians of Spanish architecture, including
the distinguished Dr Lampérez, with the primitive Segovian castle.
However, new evidence[3] indicates that the castle-palace of Real de
Manzanares was built in the second part of the fifteenth century by a

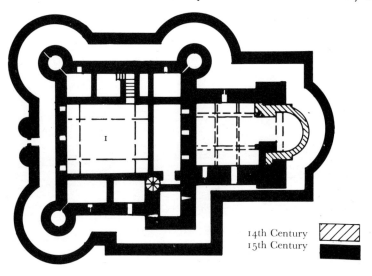

I Inner Ward

14th Century
15th Century

Ground Plan
(*from* Arquitectura Civil Española *by V.
Lamperez y Romea*)
1 Inner Ward

son of Don Iñigo, who had received in 1475 the title of Duke of the
Infantado, one of the most illustrious in Spain, from their Catholic
majesties. A low walled enclosure, the remains of the first castle, can
still be seen today at a short distance from the new castle. This castle
of Real de Manzanares, showing *Mudéjar* and late Gothic influences,
was given a basic rectangular lay-out similar to the early Segovian
fortress, to which a chapel was added on the eastern side, incorporating
parts of an ancient hermitage with its apse. Towards 1480, the second
Duke of the Infantado added the beautiful gallery, in a late Gothic
style called *Isabelino*, on the southern façade; this is the best example
of its kind in Spain.

The gallery's architect was Juan de Guas, believed to have come
originally from Lyon, who had designed the church of San Juan de los
Reyes in Toledo. This church was begun in 1476 by Ferdinand and
Isabella to commemorate the victory of Toro over the King of Portugal.
However, the castle was left unfinished. Originally a classic castle-
palace with strong outer defences protecting a luxurious palace inside,
Manzanares had a curtain wall with abundant gun-loops (in the form

[3] See Federico Bordejé's study of this castle in
Castles Itinerary in Castile. Madrid, 1965.

of long slits with two crosslet slits near the top and a circular opening at the bottom) and a fortified gate flanked by twin towers. Once inside the middle ward, the visitor entered the palace through a door on the southern façade which was covered from the keep. The castle, however, was clearly conceived in defiance of their Catholic majesties' desire to stop the building of castellated structures in Spain. Therefore, after the death of the first Duke of the Infantado, work seems to have continued only on the decorative aspects of the castle. It was at this time that the courtyard was given its columns and arches adorned with the coat-of-arms of the Mendoza, Enríquez and Luna families. It may be that the coats-of-arms carved on the towers, blackened now by the elements, also represented these proud Castilian families.

The castle of Real de Manzanares is presently under restoration. In the course of this work many important facets of its unique past are coming to light, including the lay-out of the soldiers' quarters, the well, and, in the chapel, what appears to be the remains of thirteenth-century paintings belonging originally to the ancient hermitage.

Manzanares is considered the best ornamented among Spanish castles: the only comparable building is the Andalucian castle-palace of the Marquis de Vélez Blanco (1506–15), where the main courtyard was ornamented with Renaissance marble carvings. These can now be seen at the Metropolitan Museum of Art in New York City, where they have been carefully reassembled.

Located on the Guadarrama hills near Madrid, Manzanares is believed to have been considered by Philip II as a possible site for a monastery he intended to build as an *ex-voto* for the victory of San Quintin. In fact Philip chose another site for his ambitious project which finally materialized as the famous Escorial.

El Real de Manzanares : the main gate and western façade.

SAN MARTIN DE VALDEIGLESIAS

Carefully reconstructed by its present owner, the Baron de Sacro Lirio, the castle of San Martin de Valdeiglesias is a small and compact fortress. Isabella of Castile is associated with this castle, since she was recognized as sole heiress to the throne of Castile by Henry IV in the presence of the Castilian nobility gathered at Guisando, two miles away. This decision doomed her rival, La Beltraneja, to a sad life of intrigue and unfulfilled hopes that was to end finally in a Portuguese convent.

San Martín de Valdeiglesias: the gateway.

The castle has a square keep and round corner towers with the remains of crenellations. Its entrance is protected by twin crenellated towers and a portcullis and leads through the curtain wall to a charming central courtyard, tastefully restored today. This strong castle, dating from the fifteenth century, was given by King John II of Castile to his ambitious and powerful favourite and adviser, Don Alvaro de Luna. The castle's origins, however, are unknown.

VILLAREJO DE SALVANES

Villarejo de Salvanes: ruins of the keep.

Nothing remains of this castle except its imposing keep, which dates from the fifteenth century. Today (1966) even this elegant structure, supported by eight slender towers that give it a unique geometrical appearance, is in danger of collapse.

To the traveller going South from Madrid, the keep appears to be more in the tradition of the Northern European fortified towers; but its appearance is deceptive, since it lacks a system of defence. This role was obviously fulfilled by a wall of enceinte, today totally lost. Its door, however, is at a considerable height from the ground, with rough steps leading up to it.

Villarejo de Salvanés belonged to the Military Orders and housed their Special Tribunal. As previously mentioned, one of its Masters was Don Luis de Requesens, who fought with Don Juan of Austria in the famous battle of Lepanto.

CHINCHON

The once powerful fortress of the Counts of Chinchón houses today an *anis* distillery. This unworthy fate is not unique in Europe, where castles have been transformed into breweries (in Germany) or have been bought, as in many excellent cases of military architecture in Tuscany, by Chianti producers. The requirements of industry do not

Chinchón: the main gateway to the castle, surmounted by the coat-of-arms of the Counts of Chinchón.

always coincide with those of history and architecture and the castle of Chinchón is today painfully mutilated. A visit to it, however, will be rewarding as, even in its present state, it is a good example of a castle-palace of the fifteenth century.

A draw-bridge across a deep moat, replaced today by a masonry structure, gave access to Chinchón. It was built to a square plan with the keep on the north-western corner and heavily plinthed towers at the other corners. They were about twice their present height, but otherwise the external aspect of the walls and towers is good. A central courtyard or *patio de armas* gave light to rooms for servants and soldiers which opened on to it, while the keep, which must have been three storeys high, provided spacious quarters for the Master and possibly housed a chapel. Already standing at the time when artillery came into use, Chinchón had several cannon for its defence, and thus can be classified as a transitional castle, such as Las Navas del Marqués and Villaviciosa de Odón, mentioned elsewhere in this book.

During the War of the Spanish Succession, the castle was occupied by the Austrians in 1706. When they abandoned it, the structure was stripped of its artillery and eventually a fire completed the work of destruction. The coat-of-arms of the Counts of Chinchón carved above the entrance seems to have resisted these calamities and can still be seen today.

ALCALA DE HENARES

Alcalá de Henares: the city wall and to near the Madrid gateway.

This important walled city is about twenty miles east of Madrid. Its history goes back to the Arab invasions, since a Moslem *alcazaba* was erected there. With the Reconquest of Castile, Alcalá de Henares became an important fief of the Church and the great Cardinal Cisneros proceeded to complete and expand the construction of ramparts begun in the fifteenth century by the bellicose Archbishop Tenorio of Toledo. The following century was an important period in the development of the city, not only because Cisneros built thick walls and crenellated square towers to protect it, but also because it became the cradle of a University that was to expand into an important centre of learning in the centuries to come.

The famous Palace of the Bishops has managed to withstand the ravages of time and stands proudly today. However, the state of the city's walls in parts is poor, giving an impression of total dilapidation, particularly near the eighteenth-century gate where the road from Madrid enters the city.

VILLAVICIOSA DE ODON

This imposing castle-palace, located about twelve miles from Madrid, was built in 1583 by Don Diego Fernández de Cabrera, adviser to Philip II, under the supervision of the famous architect Juan de Herrera. Of square plan with typically massive towers, Villaviciosa had a sentinel walk around the top floor, protected by crenellations. This castle replaced the one built by the Counts of Chinchón in the fifteenth century and burnt during the War of the Comuneros in 1520.

The castle played a part in the defeat of the Austrian General Stahrenberg in 1710 when Spanish reinforcements, concealed within its thick walls until the last moment, tilted the balance decisively in favour of Philip V's troops led by the Duke of Vendôme.

In one of its narrow rooms Ferdinand VI, showing signs of incipient madness, died in 1759 and eventually the castle became a political prison. Years later Villaviciosa de Odón became the property of Manuel Godoy, Prince of La Paz and powerful favourite at the court of Charles IV.

A perfect example of the unscrupulous social climber, Manuel Godoy, who was jailed eventually in his own palace, has given great pleasure to historians. J. Christopher Herold describes as follows the relationship between the Prince of La Paz and Queen Maria Luisa, the ugly wife of Charles IV of Spain: ' Her husband's hasty, frequent and therapeutic embraces left her [the Queen] unsatisfied, and she took as a lover a young guardsman, Manuel Godoy, who served her better and whom she gradually propelled into the post of chief minister. Maria Luisa ruled the king and Godoy ruled Maria Luisa, whom he treated with brutal and coarse contempt.' [4] Godoy was given the title of Prince of the Peace in 1795, for concluding the peace of Basle with France, and for years he was the real ruler of Spain. But, as a result of Napoleonic intrigues in 1808, Maria Luisa's son was crowned Ferdinand VII of Spain. One of the first actions of the new monarch was to send the Prince of the Peace to prison. The place chosen for this

[4] *The Age of Napoleon.* New York.

was Villaviciosa de Odón.

Manuel Godoy's imprisonment was harsh but brief. He occupied the oratory, a dark chamber, enlivened only by a beautiful tiled panel, that can still be seen today. He received no visitors, with the sole exception of a military surgeon who treated him for a wound on his forehead. Released at midnight on April 20, 1808, by direct intercession of Napoleon, the ex-Prince of the Peace took the road to France and to exile from which he never returned.

Villaviciosa de Odón, so close to Madrid on the route that runs west towards San Martin de Valdeiglesias, deserves special attention. It is, like the castle of Las Navas del Marqués in the province of Avila, an interesting example of a structure adapted for the use of early artillery. This concern with military matters, however, does not exclude a strong Renaissance flavour. In this, Villaviciosa is a classic example of a transitional castle. At the time of its construction, the Reconquest was long past, and the internal wars of the fifteenth century were almost settled. Its massive style was therefore tempered by elegant details. Built to three plans, with a great staircase and a square courtyard surrounded by porticos, Villaviciosa is one of Juan de Herrera's masterpieces.

THE PROVINCE OF TOLEDO

The province of Toledo, embodying the power and splendour of Castile, was the centre of the Visigothic kingdom that was destroyed at Guadelete in 711 with the Arab invasion. Toledo, which was to become the Imperial City during Charles V's reign, was the Visigothic capital. It was here that King Reccared was baptised in the Catholic faith in 589.

When the Arabs consolidated their rule over most of the Peninsula, Toledo, known as Toleitola, was defended by a powerful *alcazaba* and became a major stronghold. Its reconquest in 1085 by King Alfonso VI marked an important event in the bloody and indecisive war waged between Christians and Moslems, since it was the first major Saracen city to be wrested back and held indefinitely, even against the tremendous onslaught of the Almorávides in the twelfth century.

The Imperial City deserved its name. During the Middle Ages Toledo was one of the most heavily fortified cities in Europe. Although

Alcázar of Toledo: the coat-of-arms of Charles V above the main gate.

PROVINCE OF TOLEDO

it did not have the unity of construction that distinguishes Avila in Spain, Carcassonne and Aigues-Mortes in France, or Visby in the Swedish island of Gotland, Toledo was a well defended walled city and is today the most imposing combination of art and architecture in Spain. Its old walls are the combined work of generations of masons of Roman, Visigothic, Moslem and Christian origin. It is, however, the superb craftsmanship of the Arabs that we appreciate the most today in parts such as the Gate of Visagra. Their influence blends with that of the Imperial architects of the Hapsburg dynasty, who introduced the Renaissance style in Castile when they created the massive gate of Charles V with its twin towers adapted for the use of, and defence against, sixteenth-century artillery. Within the city walls, the Alcázar of Toledo originally formed a part of these defences. Restored during the time of the Hapsburgs, it can be said to have embodied the splendour of that epoch. Across the Tagus, the ancient fortress of San Servando, for a while the fief of the Knights Templar, adds a Gothic touch; its heavy ramparts defended the northern approach to the city.

The rest of the province was defended by a strong chain of castles that included Escalona, on the Alberche river, Maqueda, and further south the important fortresses of Montalbán, Guadamur and Consuegra.

The Bridge of San Martín crossing the Tagus.

THE BRIDGES OF ALCANTARA & SAN MARTIN

The present bridge of Alcántara was built by the Arabs in 866 on ancient Roman foundations. In spite of several attempts at restoration, the bridge has kept a Moorish flavour to this day. Alcántara, protected by the imposing castle of San Servando nearby, and San Martín to the south, were the two Toledo bridges across the Tagus. The northern road from Magerit (Madrid) led directly to the Alcázar of Toledo, passing through the strong walls that were the city's first line of defence. The bridge itself was protected by towers at both ends. The portcullis of one is still visible.

The bridge of San Martín also dates from the period of the Moorish domination of Toledo, but it was rebuilt in the fourteenth century. Its two gates, defending the narrow bridge itself, are still imposing today. The southern tower, which prevented the Arab marauders from the *taifa* kingdoms of Al-Andalus from crossing the Tagus, is an excellent example of *Mudéjar* work. The Gate of Visagra and the *Puerta del Sol*, or Gate of the Sun, in the city walls, are the most notable examples of this style in Toledo.

The Bridge of Alcántara.

SAN SERVANDO

The origin of this castle goes back to the Romans, who built a *castrum* or fortified place on the northern banks of the Tagus to defend a bridge built on the site of the present bridge of Alcántara. Centuries later, the Arabs used this same position to guard the access to their city of Toleitola, as they called the capital of Visigothic Spain, now Toledo. With the reconquest of Toledo in 1085 by Alfonso VI, San Servando was transformed into a Benedictine monastery under the rule of Cluny. Its monks come from Sahagún in northern Spain, and France.

San Servando is mentioned several times in the poem of *Myo Cid*, the anonymous Castilian epic of the twelfth century mentioned earlier in this book in connection with the castles of Atienza and Gormaz. The hero, Ruy Diaz de Vivar, was a visitor to the royal court of King Alfonso VI, the reconqueror of Toledo, in the period between 1085 and his death in 1099. The poem tells the story of his stay in the then monastery of San Servando that was burned down shortly after his death. The Cid spent some time at San Servando during the last years of his life. The particular night mentioned in the following extract of the poem is followed by a passage describing the morning when the Cid plans to visit the royal court at Toledo and instructs his men to prepare themselves. It was, one assumes, a day like many others in the life of an eleventh-century Christian warrior; the unknown poet who sung his praises had a keen eye for detail:

> 136
> The King has turned
> and started towards Toledo;
> my Cid did not wish
> to cross the Tagus that night ...
>
> ... Return as you will, my Lord
> into the city,
> and I with my men
> shall lodge in San Servando.
>
> 137
> ... Put on your armour
> over padded tunics,
> put on your breastplates
> white as the sun;
> furs and ermines
> over your breastplates,
> and draw the string tight
> that your weapons be not seen;
> under your cloaks
> gird the sweet keen swords;
> in this manner
> I would go to court,
> to demand justice
> and say what I must say.[1]

[1] From *The Poem of the Cid*, a verse translation by W. S. Merwin. London, 1959.

King Alfonso VI, who was extremely well disposed towards Ruy Diaz de Vivar at the beginning of his reign in 1072, was influenced by the jealousy of some of his vassals and banished the Cid from his realm nine years later. The Cid, a soldier of fortune, served the Count of Barcelona first, and then the Moorish *taifa* of Saragossa. However, with the disastrous defeat of Alfonso VI in the battle of Sagrajas, Almoravid power in Spain became a real danger threatening the existence of Castile. So the Cid was recalled, reinstated in the royal favour, and then proceeded to counter-attack the Moorish armies, penetrating into Al-Andalus as far as Valencia. King Alfonso, in his desperate attempt to check the Almoravid invasion, was constantly supported by the magnificent warrior and his followers. However, the Cid's popularity with the jealous king suffered more than one eclipse. This uneven relationship was due in part to the Cid's unbearable tendency to win his battles, while Alfonso was defeated successively at Jaén, Consuegra and Uclés. The Cid, already a living legend, continued to give successful battle to the Moors until his death in Valencia in 1099.

The year of the Cid's death saw a massive attack on Toledo by the Almorávides, but they failed to take the city. The Moslem army retaliated by laying waste the countryside, and eventually succeeded in setting fire to the monastery of San Servando. Patiently, King Alfonso VI rebuilt it and fortified it with curtain walls and a moat. During the twelfth century the monks suffered not only Moslem attacks and raids but also the effects of constant upheavals and rebellions caused by political power struggles within the walls of Toledo itself. As a result, they were finally forced to abandon the fortified monastery. King Alfonso VII then granted it to the Order of the Templars. Little is known of the Templar's influence in this place, although we must assume that they not only retained the monks' cloisters, but that also, bearing in mind their known capacity as castle-builders, they added the necessary fortifications to defend it, with walls of enceinte and a keep. Nothing, however, has remained of this Templar fortress and we only know for sure that the Knights left it when their Order was dissolved in the fourteenth century.

In mediaeval Castile, the military power and the wealth of the Church and some of its prelates was, at times, superior to that of the Crown. This power was expressed in the building of castles such as Turégano, Sigüenza, Coca and many others. The present castle of San Servando was also built on the instructions of a prelate, the Archbishop of Toledo, Pedro Tenorio, who rebuilt the ruins of the Templar castle in the fifteenth century. The main influence in its reconstruction was *Mudéjar*, the Gothic-Arab style prevalent in the city of Toledo as a whole and in the bridge of Alcántara in particular.

San Servando, Toledo's main bulwark as in so many previous centuries, has a powerful curtain wall with typical square pointed merlons in *Mudéjar* style, and crenellated round towers. These have narrow balconies of exquisite Arab design supported on elaborate corbels. A large open space on the steep banks of the Tagus, facing the postern gate, must have been intended earlier as an outer bailey or parade ground. Today it is used by the buses that carry students to the old building, now used as a training centre for members of the *Frente de las Juventudes* or Youth Front.

LAS GUADALERZAS

At a place called Los Yebenes, north-west of Consuegra, the curious visitor will be able to locate the castle of Las Guadalerzas. A succinct note in a publication of the *Asociación Española de Amigos de los Castillos*[2] indicates that this structure, of Arab origin like so many others in Castile, was used by the Knights of the Order of Calatrava as a hospital. As such, it lacks major fortifications. However, a corbelled projection above a side door may have been intended to support machicolated defences. The plan of the structure is square, with crenellated curtain walls connecting well-preserved round towers. The main feature is an enormous rectangular keep. The castle of Las Guadalerzas dates possibly from the sixteenth century. Externally it resembles the castle-palace of Arenas de San Pedro in the province of Madrid, the latter also having a large keep.

Las Guadalerzas was a gathering place and halt for the Christian troops moving south from Toledo in 1212 towards the battlefield of Las Navas de Tolosa.

BARCIENSE

Built in the second part of the fifteenth century, this fortified palace reflects the softer taste of the Neo-Reconquest period. It is of compact design, and on one façade of the main tower is carved the heraldic lion of the original owners, the Silvas, who according to Lampérez[3] erected the castle towards 1454. Bordejé, however, taking into account the decorative line of false machicolations encircling the castle and other

[2] Madrid, 1958.
[3] V. Lampérez y Romea: *Arquitectura Civil Española*. Madrid, 1922.

details, places its date of construction after the middle of the fifteenth century. It passed later to other important masters such as the Dukes of Infantado, Osuna and Pastrana, and Pope Leo XIII, who received it as part of an inheritance.

Barciense's plan is rectangular, with round towers on its western side. On the north-eastern corner a square tower, with walls of exceptional thickness, juts out diagonally. This powerful structure, its purpose unclear, was never finished. The present keep had a circular staircase that led to the ramparts. Another staircase, built in the thickness of the wall, is located near the gate, which was protected by a moat and barbican. Nothing remains of Barciense's interiors except blackened

Barciense: the square north-east tower.

holes in the walls showing the location of the beams that supported the second floor.

Half-way between Toledo and Maqueda, Barciense can be seen from the road, surrounded by sheep grazing peacefully. At sunset its pink towers become almost unreal, like a mirage on top of the hill.

ESCALONA

Escalona is among the most extensive fortified enclosures in mediaeval Spain. Its irregular shape is 1,300 feet in perimeter. Built on Arab foundations on the steep banks of the Alberche, Escalona was a vital link in the defences of Toledo. It underwent constant alterations at the hands of Moslem and Christian masons during the thirteenth, fourteenth and fifteenth centuries.

After the conquest of Escalona by Alfonso VI, the King ceded it to Diego and Domingo Alvárez, who received the *fuero* or civil rights of the village and were responsible for populating it. Their primitive castle was replaced later by another built by Manuel, brother of Alfonso X, who had received in 1281 the fief of Escalona and its bastions.[4] In turn, these possessions passed to Don Alvaro de Luna, the great political figure of the first half of the fifteenth century.

We do not know exactly when and how Escalona became the property of Don Alvaro, the ambitious statesman who, as favourite and adviser of King John II, was ' second to none of his contemporaries in valour, shrewdness and pride ' according to M. J. Quintana.[5] But we do know that Escalona was Don Alvaro's refuge when he fell from

[4] His son, the famous Don Juan Manuel, was born at Escalona a year later.
[5] *Vidas de Españoles célebres*. Colección Austral; Madrid, 1966.

favour. It was from there that he set out on the fateful journey that was to end with his beheading in Valladolid in 1453. Tradition says that, even after Don Alvaro's death, his banner was proudly displayed at Escalona where his son and his wife, Juana de Pimentel, lived in fear of royal displeasure. Later, it was also at Escalona that they stood out against Henry IV, King of Castile, who had bequeathed the castle to a new owner, Don Juan Pacheco, Marquis of Villena and Master of the Order of Santiago. Escalona was finally taken in 1470 in the presence of the King.

But Escalona lived through happier times, particularly from 1435–7 when, according to the Chronicle of Don Alvaro, innumerable tournaments and banquets were held there. The ruins still show a

few traces of the character of this enormous structure, built in the Castilian tradition of the fifteenth century. The work of anonymous artisans had endowed Escalona with a strong feeling of power and magnificence; but the lazy river below now reflects only the image and the spirit of an epoch, distorted by acts of violence and centuries of neglect.

The castle of Escalona had an ancient outer rampart supported by eight strong towers and defended by a moat spanned by a draw-bridge. Inside these defences was the palace, of square plan with a cloistered courtyard, and separated from the vast *plaza de armas* by another moat. Escalona's outer towers were detached from the wall in typical Moorish fashion—a style found in some castles of the Military Orders. The

torre albarrana as it was known, of Saracen origin, appears in greatly differing castles from Alcalá de Guadaira near Seville to Calatrava La Vieja near Ciudad Real; examples date from the thirteenth or beginning of the fourteenth centuries. Escalona has three well-preserved examples of the *torre albarrana*, which were linked to the roof of the fifteenth-century palace by massive arches.

Escalona's style was a blend of Gothic and *Mudéjar*. The door of the palace is an exceptional example of Gothic influence with a bas-relief on the tympan representing Don Alvaro de Luna's arms, while the interiors had extremely fine *Mudéjar* decorations. These were in stucco of detailed geometrical shapes covering areas of wall around the doors and windows. The whole structure must have been most impressive before its destruction in 1808 by French troops under General Suchet. By then, however, the castle-palace had already seen its best days, when it was one of the most luxurious in Spain.

Lampérez mentioned the remains of Escalona's small chapel, which had a square plan and an elaborate Gothic vault brightly decorated with golden and polychrome designs. He also remarked upon the motif of a cross surrounded by ten symbolic shells that represented the Order of Santiago and its Master, Don Alvaro de Luna. Unfortunately, the visitor today is confronted by a building in an appalling state of decay. A feeling of futility seems to float over the vast ruins of Escalona as it keeps a silent and useless vigil a hundred feet above the Alberche.

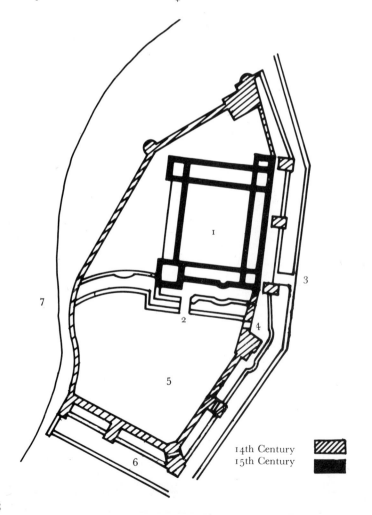

14th Century
15th Century

ESCALONA
(*from* Fortalezas y Castillos de la Edad Media *by F. Navarro*)
Ground Plan
1 Inner Ward
2 Bridge
3 Bridge
4 Main Door
5 Outer Ward
6 Moat
7 Alberche River

Right
Escalona: torre albarrana *from the moat.*

GUADAMUR

This castle-palace, one of the best preserved in Castile, was restored by the Count of Asalto, whose coat-of-arms can be seen on the impressive Gothic gate, protected by a moat and a draw-bridge.

Guadamur was built in the middle of the fifteenth century by Pedro Lopez de Ayala, the first Count of Fuensalida. Its plan is rectangular, with an outer wall supported by towers and redans.

The main body of the castle, built around a courtyard which is today covered with a glass roof, was originally two storeys high. It included the keep at the south-western corner and circular corner towers. The entrance to the middle-ward was through a long passage built in the keep itself. Towards the end of the fifteenth century, Guadamur received an additional storey, clearly defined by the recessed platform running around the castle. A storey was also added to the keep, increasing its height and thus providing the necessary mass to balance the enlarged main structure. The interesting machicolated work which crowned the imposing *torre del homenaje*, and was left unfinished, dates from this period.

Escalona: relief above the main doorway.

This residence of kings, which perhaps glimpsed one of the rare moments of happiness in the troubled lives of Philip the Handsome and his wife Joanna, became a neglected ruin in the nineteenth century. It was saved by the Count of Asalto, and today this sombre and powerful structure can be admired in all its splendour.

ALCAZAR OF TOLEDO

The famous siege during the 1936–39 Civil War resulted in the destruction of the Alcázar, so what we see today is almost entirely a reconstruction. The history of the Alcázar has always been one of destruction and restoration, beginning in the reign of Alfonso VI who, after reconquering Toledo from the Moors, built the first Alcázar on foundations provided by earlier Roman, Visigothic and Arab masons. An ancient tradition suggests that the original Christian fortress was given by Alfonso VI to the great warrior Rodrigo Diaz de Vivar, the Cid, who stationed a thousand men there.

Enlarged by Alfonso X and Peter I of Castile, the Alcázar served at one time as a prison for Queen Blanca of Bourbon, wife of Peter I. Peter also used it as a residence for his mistress, Doña Maria Padilla. Charles V transformed the Alcázar into a massive palace where his court settled for a brief period in the middle of the sixteenth century. However, it was Philip II and his architect Herrera who gave the Alcázar the character that has been kept in its latest reconstruction. Herrera's influence was particularly noticeable on the southern façade which is contemporary to the famous Escorial, his masterpiece which combines a palace with a convent and a church.

When the royal court finally moved to Madrid in 1561, the Alcázar was doomed to a secondary role and eventually became a prison. Burnt by Austrian troops under General Stahrenberg during the civil war of the eighteenth century—the War of the Spanish Succession— the Alcázar was rebuilt by Ventura Rodriguez, Charles III's architect. Its fate, however, was to be burnt again, this time at the hands of the French invaders during the Napoleonic wars. The fire lasted three days and left only the outer walls and part of the chapel designed by Herrera. Eventually the Alcázar, after considerable rebuilding, became successively a Casa de Caridad (almshouse), a Military College and finally the Academy of Infantry. In this last capacity it remained unchanged for almost fifty years until 1936, when, during the early stages of the Civil War, General Moscardó with 500 cadets, miscellaneous troops, and civilians successfully defended the Alcázar during a four-month siege. Unfortunately, extensive mining operations and field-gun bombardments finally caused its almost total ruin.

Rebuilt today with considerable care, the Alcázar of Toledo reflects in its exterior the spirit of the Counter-Reformation, not only in the typical towers with their slate-covered pointed roofs, so much admired by Philip II in Flanders, but also in the stonework on the façades. Inside, the courtyard by Covarrubias, and the monumental staircase, designed by Villapando (closely advised by the indefatigable Philip II), remind the visitor of the palace's peak of splendour in the sixteenth century.

The Alcázar, in spite of its heroic stand in the Civil War, is not a transitional fortress like other buildings designed or influenced by Herrera, such as Las Navas del Marqués. Here the emphasis was on creating a suitable residence for the Hapsburg monarchs. As such, it is a royal palace and its splendid courtyard is only slightly reminiscent of the military *patio de armas* of so many Spanish castles. With the Alcázar designed by Herrera, late Renaissance architecture was finally

The fortified city wall of Toledo.

established in Spain. The cycle which had begun with the early Arab *alcazabas* in the eighth century, proceeded to the great Spanish castles of the Middle Ages, then to the daring *castillos roqueros* of the fourteenth century, and to the castle-palaces of the Spanish nobility and transitional castles of the sixteenth century, was finally completed with the Alcázar of Toledo. This structure is in itself a glorious chapter in the history and architecture of Spain.

Alcázar of Toledo: seen from San Servando.

Toledo: the Charles V Gate.

SPANISH MILITARY ORDERS

On the battlefield of Las Navas de Tolosa in 1212 the Christian soldiers, once their victory became apparent, intoned a Te Deum to thank God for their triumph. They were joined in this spontaneous expression of thanks by the Kings Alfonso VIII of Castile, Sancho V of Navarre, Peter II of Aragón, and by the Archbishops of Toledo and Narbonne. The presence of the clergy on the battlefields of the Reconquest was not fortuitous. The Church was a vital factor in the war against the Infidels and its representatives had to inject new enthusiasm into the failing hopes or the sudden despair of the Christian kings exposed to the constant trials of a war that lasted more than seven centuries.

This aspect was particularly true of the Holy War after the defeat of Alarcos, a great and final Almohade victory in Spain. At that time, the same archbishop of Toledo who was present at Las Navas, Don Rodrigo Jiménez de Rada, was a powerful instrument in the preparation of the new Christian army that was eventually gathered at Toledo for the momentous march to the South. Organizing this army was no small undertaking, it was the largest ever assembled until that time, including 60,000 knights and mounted warriors from many parts of Spain, as well as contingents from France, Germany and other European states. It was, in fact, the result of a new Crusade, preached by Jiménez de Rada and sanctioned by the Pope.

A religious element had been present in Spain since the eighth century when the first counter-attacks against the invading Arabs took place. It spread in Europe, resulting in the Crusades, and culminated in the creation of the Military Orders. These were militant bodies of brothers, bound by religious vows, who took upon themselves certain specific tasks connected with the propagation of the faith. To bear arms became eventually a specific part of their duties and, as a result, the religious Orders became military Orders, though they never lost sight of their spiritual origin. From Jerusalem, where the Order of the Hospitalers (the Knights of St John) was created in 1113 by special dispensation of Pope Pascal II, this Order and that of the Templars created shortly thereafter, extended their influence to Spain. King Alfonso I of Aragón, for one, was strongly influenced by them, while Berenguer III, King of Barcelona, died in the robes of a Knight Templar. In the second part of the twelfth century, however, the foreign Orders inspired the foundation of purely Spanish counterparts, the Military Orders of Calatrava, Santiago and Alcántara.

Some historians have adopted the attitude that the Spanish military Orders were simply a complement of the foreign Orders already fighting in Spain and, in a way, indicated a nationalistic reaction against Templar and Hospitaler knights, mostly of French origin. Were the Spanish Orders then mere copies of those that appeared in

Arms and armour in the Alcázar of Segovia.

the Holy Land at the time of the Crusades? This seems to be an over-simplification and Américo Castro in his admirable work *The Structure of Spanish History*[1] has drawn attention to the fact that *all* the Orders which combined a fighting spirit with a religious one appeared as an answer to similar institutions created by the Arabs: 'It is not a matter of chance' he says, 'that the Orders were born in the twelfth century in lands that were Christian outposts against Islam: Palestine and Spain.'

Although it was accepted in the Moslem world, the possibility of leading simultaneously a religious and martial existence was an alien and contradictory concept for a Christian. None other than Bernard de Clairvaux (the future St Bernard), the man eventually chosen by Louis VII of France and Pope Eugene III to preach the Second Crusade at Vézelay in 1146, was needed to make the European clergy accept the Order of the Knights Templar. His famous sermon *De laude novae militiae*, written at the request of the first Master of the Order, Hugh de Paynes, opened the door for the approval of its statutes by the Council of Troyes in 1128.

The first of the Orders to appear in the Holy Land was that of the Hospitalers, which took care of the sick pilgrims who visited Jerusalem. Shortly afterwards, the Templars, defined as *pauperi commilitones Christi*, were created to defend the pilgrims en route to the Holy City against the attacks of the Saracens. Once the knights were accepted in their

[1] Princeton, 1954.

role of protectors of the Faith through violence (like their counterparts, the Murabits or Almorávides), their power grew rapidly. The high point in their prestigious role as bulwarks of the Christian faith in the Levant was reached during the latter part of the twelfth century, when the Templars and Hospitalers became the only permanent and regular forces employed against Islam. However, their position in Europe itself was relatively tenuous. Accepted as long as they fought the Infidels, the military Orders lost their status as holy warriors when they were unable to prevent the reconquest of Palestine by the Saracens, who succeeded in taking St John of Acre at the end of the thirteenth century.

When the knights returned to France, their religious origin was overlooked in favour of more mundane considerations. The Order of the Hospitalers, from their new and strategic base established in Cyprus, became an important naval power, while the Order of the Knights Templar became a commercial enterprise, controlling for more than two centuries the trade route between Western Europe and the Orient. These knights became bankers, accumulating enormous riches in the process. Soon they were too powerful to be left alone, and Philip the Handsome destroyed the political aspirations of the Order at the beginning of the fourteenth century. Using as a pretext the final disappearance of Christian influence in Palestine, the king took prisoner the Grand Master of the Order, Jacques de Molai, and many of his knights. The confessions of the Knights Templar, disclosing secret, blasphemous initiation rites and other crimes, led to the dissolution of the Order by Pope Clement V in 1312 at the Council of Vienne. With the hasty execution at the stake of Jacques de Molai and one of his commanders, Philip finally secured possession of the Order's wealth on March 18, 1314.

As Américo Castro points out, in France the inability of the Order to make a neat division between heaven and earth, faith and reason, led the knights to their logical fate: death, since the French mind could not tolerate contradictions for very long. As in France, similar inquiries into the Military Orders were held in England, Germany, Italy and Spain. Confessions of impiety and even immorality were obtained in all countries, except Spain. There the Templars, ensconced in their redoubts, stubbornly resisted the King of Aragón, but were finally overwhelmed and thrown into prison. A similar fate befell them in Castile. There they were arrested and tried before an ecclesiastical tribunal, but eventually were declared innocent. What could not be tolerated in other lands, namely their mixture of mysticism and worldliness, in fact enabled the Military Orders to survive in Spain.

The immediate impetus for the creation of the truly original Spanish Orders was the powerful irruption in 1086 of the fanatical Almorávides in southern Spain. Led by holy warriors who lived in ascetic communities called *rábidas*, the Almoravid armies put new blood and decision into the tottering small kingdoms or *taifas* that had replaced the Caliphate of Cordoba after its disintegration in 1031. The mystical power of the Almorávides was clearly understood on the Christian side and led eventually to the creation of similar military brotherhoods following the patterns of the Templars and Hospitalers. The first of the Spanish Orders was that of Calatrava, which made a strong impact on the history of Spain by its heroic resistance to the Almoravid inroad.

Before describing the birth of this and other Orders, it is important to mention that the Templars and Hospitalers not only provided an adequate example for the Spanish Orders, but were also instrumental in bringing to Spain new methods of war and defence. Their magnificent fortresses in the Holy Land, such as Krak des Chevaliers, built by the Hospitalers (who had in turn absorbed the lessons imposed by their Islamic enemies), appeared all over Western Europe and eventually in Spain. Typical of the Eastern Orders' influence was the castle of Ponferrada in the province of León, strategically located on the *camino de Santiago*, as the route of the pilgrims from France to Santiago de Compostela was called during the Middle Ages. In existence from the time of the Romans, Ponferrada was given by the kings of León to the Knights Templar in 1178 and underwent extensive repairs that transformed it into a truly Gothic fortress of which extensive ruins remain today.

page 195
Calatrava La Nueva: the castle hall with barrel-vaulted ceiling and ventilation slits above the door.

Calatrava La Vieja

The second part of the twelfth century was certainly a prosperous time for the Templars, since, following the example of Alfonso I of Aragón, who had in 1134 named them heirs of his kingdom, the knights received generous subsidies from the successive kings of Castile. In proportion to the slow tide of the Reconquest, the Templars were given new towns and properties with the duty of defending them against the Moors. Such was the case with the fortress of Calat-rabat (castle on the plain) an Arab bastion on the banks of the Guadiana river, conquered by Alfonso VII in 1147. Located between Toledo and Córdoba, Calat-rabat or Calatrava, as it was eventually known by the Christians, was defended by the Templars for ten years against repeated attacks by Moorish chieftains. A weakening of the knights' martial

Opposite
Calatrava La Nueva: the walls seen from the inner ward.

spirit after the death of Alfonso VII led directly to the creation of the Order of Calatrava. When the Templars informed Alfonso's successor, Sancho III, that 'they could not withstand the great power of the Arabs', the king offered Calatrava, the open gap in the defences of his realm, to whoever would dare to resist the Moorish onslaught. This desperate gamble produced results: a Cistercian monk (from the Benedictine Order reformed by St Bernard), Fray Raimundo de Fitero, together with Diego Vázquez, who had earlier fought with Alfonso VII's army, accepted the challenge. However, Fray Raimundo requested, as a condition for their defence of Calatrava, that he should be allowed to create a new Military Order. The King accepted this

condition, naming Fray Raimundo Captain General of the Order of Calatrava. The agreement is mentioned for the first time in 1158, when Sancho III gave the fortress of Calatrava to Fray Raimundo de Fitero '*ut defendatis eam a paganis inimicis crucis Christi*' and to whom in the future might be '*vestri ordinis et ibi Deo servire voluerint*'. Subject to Benedictine rules, the Order was eventually confirmed in Rome by Pope Alexander III in 1164.

However, on the death of Fray Raimundo, the monks returned to their cloisters and the knights became independent from the Cistercian Order. The Order of Calatrava, which now joined the Crusade against the Moors, acquired its own castles and founded its own monasteries. Manzanares, Benavente, Maqueda, Ciruelos, Zorita de los Canes and Anguix were among those garrisoned by this powerful Order. Their original stronghold, the castle of Calatrava (called *la Vieja*) eventually fell to the Almohades led by Ibn-Yusef who forced the knights to retreat south to the castle of Salvatierra. There the Order tried to consolidate its position and managed to hold the castle

Right

Calatrava La Nueva: main façade of the chapel showing the rose-window.

for a decade, until it, too, was captured by the Almohades.

After Salvatierra was forced to surrender the surviving knights found a new refuge in the castle of Zorita de los Canes on the banks of the Tagus. Only after the battle of Las Navas de Tolosa in 1212 could the Order of Calatrava regain control of the region round the Guadiana river. Eventually they built the fortified convent of Calatrava *la Nueva* close to the old castle of Salvatierra. From there the Order continued its fight against the Moors who, however, never fully recovered from their defeat at Las Navas de Tolosa.

The Orders of Santiago and Alcántara followed the pattern set by Calatrava. According to the previously mentioned Rodrigo Jiménez de Rada, Archbishop of Toledo (1180(?)–1247) who wrote *De rebus Hispaniae*, Alfonso VIII established the Order of Santiago at the town of Uclés:

' *In Uclesio statuit caput ordinis,*
  et opus eorum eusis defensionis;
  persecutor Arabum moratur ibi,
  et incola eius defensor fidei;'

This decision was taken by the victor of Las Navas de Tolosa around 1174, and it implied that the Order was intended to have a definite mission ' to fight with the sword in the defence of the land '. Chronological vagueness shrouds the founding of the Order of Santiago. However, Don Angel Dotor has determined that they were originally

Right
Zorita de los Canes: the ruined gateway and
torre de las armas *from the inner ward.*

Calatrava La Vieja

known as Friars of Cáceres, under the protection of the Apostle
Santiago (St. James), and later became members of the Brotherhood
of the Friars of the Sword. Eventually the Brotherhood was transformed into the Military Order of Santiago, whose first temple and
convent was in the church of Santiago, outside the walls of Cáceres.
By 1172, the Order was already established in Castile.

In addition to fighting the Moors, the Knights of Santiago were
concerned, through a branch existing in León, with the protection of
pilgrims on their journey to Santiago de Compostela. The Knights'
emblem was a red sword in the form of a cross and the war-like Archbishop Rodrigo de Rada naturally said that it was red because it was

'dyed in the blood of the Arabs' The Order of Santiago also adopted another symbol, that of the shell, which was the emblem of the Saint and martyr, Santiago, whose shrine was venerated at Santiago de Compostela.

It was this shrine which attracted the thousands of pilgrims from all over Europe who followed the road to Santiago or *camino francés* as it was also known. This French road, of tremendous importance during the Middle Ages, entered Spain through the valley of the Aspe and the gorge of Somport in the Pyrenees. It was replaced later by another route passing through the valley of Roncevaux, made famous by Charlemagne and the well-known *Chanson de Roland*. The road passed

through Pamplona, Burgos and León before it reached Compostela.
In France there were clearly defined routes for the pilgrims. The Via
Turonensis, for example, passed through Tours, Poitiers and Bordeaux
and so to Paris. Santiago-bound pilgrims in Paris crossed the city by
the Rue Saint-Jacques (Santiago Street) and would congregate at the
church of Saint-Jacques-de-la-Boucherie, whose famous Tour Saint-
Jacques, in the heart of Paris, still stands today.[2]

The Knights of Santiago are presumed to have been the defenders
of the pilgrims on Spanish soil, as well as the providers of their most
immediate needs during the arduous journey. In 1175, the Order
received confirmation of its statutes from Pope Alexander III.

The third military Order originated in Extremadura in the town of
Alcántara, which was built on a powerful rock on the banks of the Tagus
and had been conquered by Alfonso VIII after a long siege in 1214.
The king gave the town to the Order of Calatrava, which transferred
it later to the Order of San Julián del Pereiro (a religious brotherhood
created in 1156 who adhered to the rules of St Benedict), on condition
that the latter would accept the tutelage of the Order of Calatrava.
The Order of Pereiro—which had, according to Dotor, the function
of protecting the Spanish/Portuguese frontier – transferred their main
monastery to Alcántara and after a papal dispensation, freed themselves

[2] *Histoire d'Espagne* by Jean Descola.

from the Order of Calatrava and created the Order of Alcántara. This Order expanded rapidly, its wealth and influence growing with the Arab retreat. In the middle of the fifteenth century its power extended to southern Spain, where its Master received from John II the superb castle of Belalcázar, near the reconquered city of Córdoba. An important castle-palace owned by the Order of Alcántara was Zalamea in the province of Cáceres. At the end of the fifteenth century Don Juan de Zuñiga, Grand Master of the Order, who was a disciple of the famous humanist Antonio de Nebrija, founded a scientific academy at Zalamea where two famous Jewish astronomers, Abraham Zacuto and Abasurto, shared their knowledge with a group of selected students.

The Orders of Montesa and San Jorge de Alfama were more localized and active particularly in Valencia. Their purpose was to garrison the castles and convents that had belonged to the Templars and Hospitalers after the dissolution of these Orders at the beginning of the fourteenth century. Together with other properties, the Order of Montesa was in charge of the tremendous castle of Peñíscola built by the Templars on the Mediterranean coast. Established by James II of Aragón in 1317, this Order appears to have been little more than a branch of the Order of Calatrava, whose statutes governed it. However, the Masters of Montesa were responsible for the administration of their Order and had powers of jurisdiction over their own knights.

With the gradual weakening of Moslem power in Al-Andalus, the military Orders began to put aside their Holy War in favour of more materialistic pursuits, such as the accumulation of wealth, and political intrigue. By the middle of the fifteenth century their decadence was manifest. This moral decay explains how someone like Don Pedro Girón could become Master of the Order of Calatrava. His political power was so great that at one point Henry IV thought of marrying young Isabella, the future Queen of Castile, to him. Townsend Miller, commenting on this episode, says: ' Marriage to the Master of Calatrava would have been a disaster of almost inconceivable proportions. Girón had one of the worst reputations in Castile. In treachery and turbulence, he equalled his brother Villena; in moral turpitude he even exceeded him.'[3]

Lope de Vega, inspired by an actual event, reflected the popular feeling against the moral decadence of the Orders in his famous play *Fuenteovejuna*: In 1476, the populace of the little town of Fuenteovejuna, in the province of Córdoba, tiring of the excesses (. . . *sin haber mujer, casada o doncella, segura a sus desmanes*) of the local *Comendador* of Calatrava, Fernán Gómez de Guzmán, attacked his palace and threw the despot through a window after killing his servants.

It would be unwise, however, to let these unfortunate later developments interfere with a due appreciation of the vital role played by the Spanish Orders in the Reconquest and their influence on all aspects of life in Mediaeval Spain. Once their Crusade was won, the Orders in many cases became the patrons of artistic and scientific enterprises. We have already mentioned the famous Master of Alcántara and Calatrava, Don Juan de Zuñiga and his support of scientific undertakings. Others worked on the same principle, for instance Don Luis de Guzmán, Grand Master of Calatrava, who wanted to read an accurate version of the Old Testament, so commissioned Rabbi Arragel of Guadalajara work on it at Maqueda for ten years.

The talent of the Orders for fortifying the frontiers of Christian

[3] *The Castles and the Crown.* New York, 1963.

Spain was centred in castles and fortified convents. We cover some of them in the following pages, such as Zorita de los Canes (Guadalajara), Anguix (Guadalajara), and Maqueda (Toledo), fiefs of the Order of Calatrava. Of them, Zorita is fully representative of their style of fortification, incorporating the extramural tower, or *torre albarrana*, which was detached from the main body of the castle except for a communicating bridge. The religious origin and purpose of the Orders was also stressed in their fortresses, where the chapel, seldom absent in a Spanish castle, grew in importance and in some cases became a true church. Both Zorita and Calatrava la Nueva have excellent examples of these developments.

During the fifteenth century, the fight for sinecures within the Orders added to the internecine struggles that characterized the anarchic period before the unification of Spain under their Catholic majesties. It was Isabella who eventually appropriated for the Crown the right to nominate the Grand Master of the Orders, and her first choice for the title was her husband, Ferdinand. Later, the King of Spain became automatically the head of the Orders. This practice began in the sixteenth century, when the Emperor Charles V was the first to receive the honour.[4]

Colour: Gormaz

Calatrava La Nueva

[4] For further information on the Spanish Military Orders see: *Capitulo General de las Ordenes Militares*. Toledo, 1560. (British Museum, Egerton MS No. 486).

CALATRAVA LA VIEJA

The original castle of the Order of Calatrava is located on the left bank of the Guadiana River, near Carrión de Calatrava. Today the venerable structure is little more than a ruin of elongated shape, distorted by years of war and eight centuries of neglect, standing amid cultivated fields. But in spite of its sad state, the first castle of Calatrava, the key to Andalucía, is still a place of considerable interest.

The castle was built on the site of an Arab *alcazaba* and had a main enclosure of irregular octagonal shape, protected by a moat which could be flooded with water from the river. A second enclosure attached to the main one—as in the Arab castle of Gormaz—was intended to protect the garrison's livestock. The wall of enceinte of the main enclosure is in general still quite well defined, except for the section which faces the marshes of Guadiana. The two most important features of the enclosure are the remains of an extramural tower or *torre albarrana* and a chapel. According to Sainz de Robles, the chapel was called ' of the Martyrs ' because it was built on the spot where those Christians who would not renounce their faith were executed by the Moslems.

The history of Calatrava la Vieja begins in the eighth century, when it is mentioned in connection with the civil wars that were troubling the recently consolidated Caliphate of Córdoba Two centuries later it had become a powerful *alcazaba* strategically placed on the road between Toledo and the capital of the Caliphate. Its purpose was to prevent the Christians from reaching the fertile lands of Andalucía which were increasingly threatened by the armies that had liberated Toledo in 1085. Eventually Alfonso VII, the Magnanimous, conquered this bastion in 1147 and gave it to the Knights Templar after converting the Arab mosque within its walls into a chapel.

For ten years the Templars successfully held Calatrava against the Moors, but, after the death of Alfonso VII, they were forced to evacuate it. Its new owners soon became a serious threat to the kingdom of

Calatrava La Vieja

209

Castile. In order to hold them back, King Sancho III offered Calatrava to any warrior who was ready and willing to defend it, and it was the courageous acceptance of his offer by Fray Raimundo de Fitero and Diego Vázquez which led to the temporary relief of Calatrava and to the eventual creation of the first Spanish Military Order.

Towards the end of the twelfth century, the Christian army suffered a bitter defeat at Alarcos. The victors were the highly disciplined Almohades led by Ibn-Yusef, and it was they who recaptured the fortress of Calatrava after a great deal of bloodshed. The Knights of the Order were forced to retreat first to Ciruelos and then to Salvatierra, about thirty miles south of Calatrava la Vieja. There they kept precarious control for ten years until, after a siege that lasted three months, they were again forced to surrender. Their defeat destroyed the power of the Order in the Ciudad Real region, but the knights were not forgotten by their king. They eventually received the castle of Zorita de los Canes in the province of Guadalajara from Alfonso VIII, and did not return to the banks of the Guadiana until after the victory of the Christian armies at Las Navas de Tolosa. The Arab defenders of Calatrava la Vieja, overwhelmed by the momentous news of the Almohade defeat, surrendered on July 1, 1212. Their lives were spared by the knights, but their own master, the Caliph of Córdoba, ordered their execution as traitors.

Once again the Order's banners flew proudly from the battered fortress of Calatrava; but it was never renovated. The Order of Calatrava chose a new location, not far from the old castle of Salvatierra, and there founded its principal residence in 1216. This became the powerful castle-convent of Calatrava la Nueva, so named to distinguish it from the ruins of Calatrava la Vieja north of Ciudad Real.

CALATRAVA LA NUEVA

One of the most important monuments of military-religious architecture in Spain, Calatrava la Nueva, was built after the victory of Las Navas de Tolosa. It was probably in about 1216 that the Order of Calatrava transferred its headquarters to the new fortress.[5] A century later, in 1317, a Papal Bull recognized the new establishment, which was to be governed by the same rules as the original Order of Calatrava. The castle had three main features which were intimately associated with the character of the Order: the keep and double walls of enceinte which rise steeply from the hill on which the castle is built; the church; and the cloister, where the warrior-monks were quartered.

The main gate, surmounted by a pointed arch of Gothic design, led through the outer walls. The entrance to the castle proper was through a massive door, and overlooking it were two elongated slits providing light and ventilation for an impressive hall with a barrel-vaulted ceiling and cobbled floor. From here, an opening gave on to the *patio de armas*.

Unlike the ramparts of the castle, the church has unfortunately lost some of its original splendour. It faces the outer defences of the fortress and a marvellous view of the Manchego countryside can be enjoyed from the vantage point of the Gothic door, reached by a flight of twelve steps. Above this door was a magnificent rose-window, but very little

[5] See Lawrence-Archer, *Orders of Chivalry*, 1887. It should also be mentioned that the Order of Calatrava suffered two periods of schism: first in 1296 when its Master, López Padilla, was opposed by an Anti-Master, Gutiérrez Pérez, and again in 1404.

of its tracery now remains. The interior of the church still shows Romanesque influence, which lends a note of toughness and severity wholly appropriate to the difficult times in which the building was constructed.

The visitor to this castle-convent follows a road that winds steadily up the hill and has been used for centuries. Philip II used it in 1560 when he visited the monument. By then, Calatrava la Nueva had already fallen into decay, closely following the fate of the Order itself. In the fifteenth century Ferdinand and Isabella attended to its restoration, but unfortunately for the last time.

Zorita de los Canes: the apse of the chapel.

ZORITA DE LOS CANES

Zorita de los Canes is one of the most impressive castles in the province of Guadalajara: the visitor is awed by its size and the strength of its ramparts. Today, Zorita is still a reminder of the skill which the Order of Calatrava developed in building its fortresses. This one, built on the site of a Moorish *alcazaba*, was given to the Order by King Alfonso VIII in 1174 after the knights had had to evacuate their castles of Calatrava la Vieja and Salvatierra, following the sustained onslaught of the Almohades.

1 Tower and Gate
2 Knights' Lodgings
3 Staircase to Underground Galleries
4 Torre Albarrana
5 Apse of Chapel
6 Nave
7 Knights' Graveyard
8 Main Tower
9 Artillery Bulwark (16th Century)
10 Artillery Position (16th Century)
11 Presumed Moat
12 Inner Ward
13 Outer Wall of Enceinte

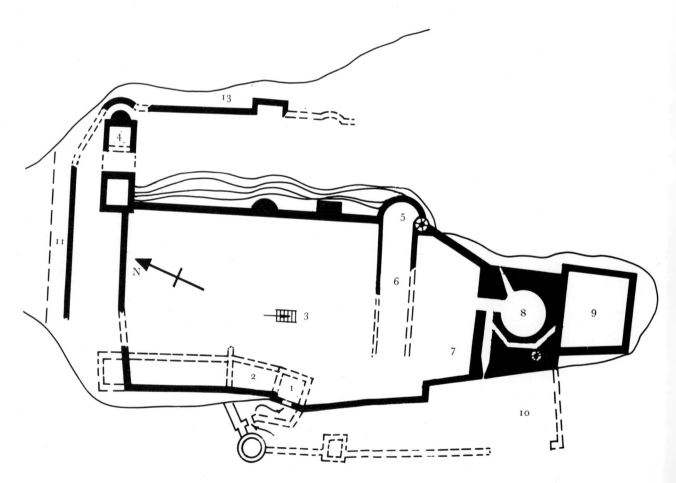

According to the Moslem chronicler, Rasis, the Arabs built a fortress on the Tagus with the stones of the destroyed Racupel, which in turn may have been the historic Recópolis, a Visigothic town built by King Leovigild in honour of his son, Reccared. In 926 the position was wrested by Abd-ar-Rahman III from the hands of a rebellious vassal. It was conquered in 1085 by Alfonso VI who gave it to the immortal Alvar Fañez, one of his subjects. The epic poem of the Cid mentions both Zorita and its Master, Alvar Fañez, among the distinguished warriors who followed the Cid: '*Albar Fañez, que Zorita mandó . . .*' (Alvar Fañez, who governed Zorita . . .).

After the bloody invasions of the Almohades in the twelfth century, Zorita fell again into Arab hands, only to be recaptured by the Christians. To secure this strategic location in the Tagus valley, which defended the access to Toledo from the East, the Order of Calatrava expanded and reinforced Zorita, transforming it into an impregnable bastion. A tradition relates that the knights kept fifty ferocious hounds to guard the fortress: hence the expression *de los canes* (of the hounds) which was added to the original name of Zorita (or Corita).

The castle occupies the top of a mound overlooking the Tagus River and is, as is so often the case in Castile, an integral part of the

Zorita de los Canes: general view from the east; on the right is the torre albarrana.

fortifications of the village of Zorita. It consisted of an outer wall of enceinte, the remains of which are still clearly visible on the north and west sides, and the castle itself. Powerful towers stood at the north-west and north-east corners, at the centre of the western wall where its entrance was located, and in the southern wall. The southern tower was the keep. There may have been a moat on the flat ground facing the northern ramparts. The rest of the circumference was protected by steep walls of calcareous rock.

A typical feature of the Calatrava castles, the *torre albarrana*, supports Zorita's north-east tower and is connected to the castle by a solid Gothic arch. The beautiful arched gate also remains today, showing clearly defined grooves for the long vanished portcullis. This thirteenth-century Gothic gate has been more or less superimposed on a much older one of Moorish origin in the shape of a horseshoe. Only the façade and an arched window remain of the gatehouse or *torre de las armas*. It is difficult to reach, because great masses of rock have fallen from the crumbling ramparts; and once the visitor has reached the gate, he is disappointingly confronted by the *patio de armas* in a state of total dilapidation. The castle was designed to contain three important basic features: lodgings for the knights of the Order, a chapel, and the

keep. The knights quarters were built of perishable materials and now black holes in the western wall mark their location. The rooms were on two storeys, and a window on the upper floor is still intact – otherwise little remains.

The chapel deserves attention. It is a perfect example of Romanesque architecture, with a barrel-vaulted nave approximately 60 feet long and 15 feet wide. Its apse today is in a reasonable state of repair. As in the case of the cathedral of Avila, where the apse was integrated in the walls of the city, the apse of Zorita's chapel was part of a powerful tower reinforcing the eastern wall of enceinte. Covered in part by ugly remains of stucco, the apse at present consists of a vault supported by four slender arches that meet at the key-stone of the arch that separates it from the nave. On the wall of the apse, graceful capitals, supporting the weight of the four arches, add a pathetic touch of elegance to the otherwise severe construction that predominates in Zorita. Adjacent to the chapel is the *corral de los condes*, a flat area that Layna Serrano assumes was the knights' churchyard. After crossing it and descending a flight of steps, the visitor enters the main tower, or *torre del homenaje*, and a vaulted room aired only by a narrow slit. Many aspects of the tower remain problematical. It is possible, for instance, that the steps did not originally exist and that the level of the *corral de los condes* was raised after the construction of the powerful tower. This would explain the ungainly descent to what must have been a key point of the castle: the room with its vault of ashlar stone, entered through a Romanesque arch. This entrance also leads, on the right, to a narrow passage cut inside the walls of the tower which communicates with the southern platform. However, before reaching this open space, the passage branches out into a spiral staircase which led to the upper floors, today no longer existing. Another passage, also built in the thickness of the wall, directly on the right of the entrance to the tower, leads to a gun-port on the western wall. This detail suggests that the keep was built, or enlarged, in the early fifteenth century.

The castle of Zorita de los Canes shows, then, Moorish, Romanesque and Gothic influences. It is not easy to put a date to this conglomeration of imposing ruins. However, an inscription on the *torre albarrana* helped to solve the mystery. It says: ' . . . Rui Diaz me fecit en . . . era de mill et CCC e XXVIII '. The year, in our present chronology, was 1290.[6] At that time the castle's defences were further reinforced by the addition of the Gothic door with its portcullis. The chapel, on the other hand, is possibly earlier.

Additional reinforcements, this time to accommodate a battery of cannon at the southern end as well as platforms for artillery on the south-west side of the castle, were carried out in the sixteenth century. However, with the withdrawal of the Knights of Calatrava during this century, the proud fortress began its decline. It passed first to the House of Pastrana and, although Philip II had stipulated in 1565, when he sold it to Ruy Gómez de Silva, that ' after two lives ' it should revert to the Order of Calatrava, the castle remained in the possession of the Dukes of Pastrana, and later of Infantado, until 1723, when ownership was transferred to the ancestors of the Counts of San Rafael.

Some interesting features of this castle are still unexplored. They include the crypt under the chapel and the underground galleries criss-crossing the rock on which the castle stands.

[6] It was in 1383 that King John I established the Christian calendar, beginning with the birth of Christ, thus making a difference of thirty-eight years between the old Roman calendar and the new system. This momentous step was taken by John I at the Alcázar of Segovia. An inscription similar to that at Zorita can be seen at the castle of Alter do Chao in Portugal: 'In the year 1359, on September 22, the very noble King D. Pedro ordered the castle of Alter do Chao to be built.' This means that it was built in 1321 according to our present calendar.

ANGUIX

A white plaque on the wall of this *castillo roquero* says: 'To King Alfonso VIII, the victor at Las Navas de Tolosa, who founded the fief of Anguix and ordered his vassal Martin Ordóñez to build this castle which earned great honour and glory.' The primitive castle of Anguix was built by Martin Ordóñez in the thirteenth century; but little remains of this original construction, replaced in the fourteenth or early fifteenth century by the present castle.

Anguix is a classical example of a *castillo roquero*. This type of military castle was common in frontier areas where mountains or steep hills encouraged the settlement of fortified outposts on almost inaccessible

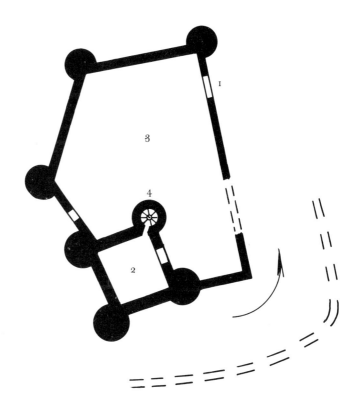

1 Main Entrance
2 Keep
3 Inner Ward
4 Spiral Staircase

rocks. These natural foundations served the dual function of giving a vantage point for observation and rendering a frontal attack almost impossible. In the case of Anguix, the walls of the castle, ten feet thick, follow the straight lines of a cliff overlooking the Tagus River. Here, the contrast with the rest of the poor and arid landscape of La Mancha is extreme, since the sparse vegetation of the countryside changes into luxurious greenery in the vicinity of the river and its nearby dam. The castle itself, of pentagonal plan dominated by the *torre del homenaje*, is compact and perfectly adapted to the dimensions of the rock that serves as its foundation.

The entrance to the castle was located near the north-east corner, with a path leading to it passing round the powerful keep. Following classical defence tradition, as the keep was the ultimate point of resistance, it was located as far as possible from the entrance and built into the wall of enceinte. Today, some portions of the eastern wall are disintegrating and have lost most of their crenellations. The keep and the remainder of the walls, made of *mamposteria* covered with limestone, are still in a relatively good state of repair.

The interiors of the keep on the other hand are lost, except for those fifteenth-century details that were an integral part of the structure. One of them was a spiral staircase, set into the north-west corner of the donjon, which led to two superimposed rooms and to the top of the tower. Other typical details were a window with side benches and a chimney built in the main room, which was on the second floor.

In addition to the well in the inner ward of the *patio de armas*, there was another in the keep. The door of the keep, another typical fifteenth-century feature, was placed above the ground-level of the inner ward. It was reached by a simple ladder which could be removed in time of danger.

The castle of Anguix depended on the nearby Zorita de los Canes and it was part of the chain of defences against the Moors established on the Tagus River. Zorita belonged to the Order of Calatrava and the Knights of this Order also garrisoned Anguix. It subsequently became the property of the Carrillo family.

During the War of the Spanish Succession at the beginning of the eighteenth century, Austrian soldiers occupied the castle; but it was eventually recaptured by Philip V's troops. Today, still looking like an Alpine stronghold, Anguix is no more than a shell, protecting only weeds, and lizards basking in the sun.

MAQUEDA

The main entrance to the castle of Maqueda is located on the north-west corner. The gate, protected from above by machicolations supported by three corbels, had an iron grill instead of a portcullis. The postern, still clearly visible today, was a Gothic opening on the eastern façade.

Located to the west of the city of Toledo, on the road that runs from Madrid to Extremadura, the castle of Maqueda was built on ancient foundations that some historians consider to be of Roman origin. During the Arab conquest, the master-mason Fatho-ben-Ibrahim, famous builder of mosques in Toledo, worked in Maqueda for the powerful Al-Mansur. Before its reconquest by Alfonso VI towards the end of the eleventh century, Maqueda witnessed a cruel spectacle. Outside the castle walls the Moslem leader Wadhah, supported by Christian warriors, defeated his rival Obeidala who was taken prisoner and received mortal knife wounds in the head, while his lieutenants were crucified on one of the towers of the castle.

The castle of Maqueda, built on a rectangular plan covering an area 215 feet long and 200 feet wide has a curtain wall which is still almost intact. This is 15 feet thick and about 50 feet high, crowned with pointed merlons of *Mudéjar* design. The strong round towers at its corners still bear an elaborate type of crenellation (although parts were recently reconstructed) which was built by Gutierre de Cárdenas in the fifteenth century.

Zorita de los Canes: window and doorway in the torre de las armas, *from the courtyard.*

[7] *Fortalezas y Castillos de la Edad Media* (Maqueda y Escalona). Madrid, 1895.

The original crenellation work is of great interest. It included openings for cross-bows and hand guns and consisted of twin merlons joined by a wall provided with an opening for observation. Inverted key-hole ports were also pierced in the parapet supporting the merlons. These openings, according to Felipe Navarro,[7] were intended only for cross-bows, since their position near the floor of the sentinel walk prevented the use of fire-arms. This type of low-positioned loop-hole was used in other Castilian structures of the fifteenth century, particularly in the castle-palace of Coca.

The tower of Vela, now almost lost among the houses of the village of Maqueda, formed part of an external wall of defence surrounding the village, and still stands today as yet another important example of Arab architecture. Built in layers of *mamposteria* (crushed stones and mortar) alternating with bricks, the tower of Vela bears a strong resemblance to similar work at the castle of Escalona, where the work of Arab and Christian masons is combined. Another similarity, this time to the famous Puerta del Sol in Toledo, indicates that the tower might be contemporary to the time when the Imperial City was at the height of its splendour in the fifteenth century. At that time Archbishop Pedro Tenorio rebuilt the castle of San Servando and some of the defences of Toledo.

The castle and village of Maqueda were given to the Military Order of Calatrava by King Alfonso VIII in 1177 and for centuries were associated with the Masters of the Order. It was in this castle that Peter the Cruel ordered the execution of the Master, Don Juan Nuñez de Prado, because of his support of the repudiated Queen, Doña Blanca. Ferdinand and Isabella made Maqueda head of the Duchy of the same name and gave it to Diego de Cárdenas. The castle today is used as barracks for the Civil Guard.

Maqueda: general view showing clearly the pointed merlons on the crenellations.

Consuegra

CONSUEGRA

Little is known of this stronghold on the southern limit of the province of Toledo, today in ruins. It belonged to the Hospitalers, members of the monastic Order of St John of Jerusalem. Consuegra reminds us of those fortresses built in Syria during the Crusades, where the Hospitalers learnt their construction techniques. The castle seems to reflect this influence, with its double walls of enceinte and a central keep with round towers. It may have included, as in Calatrava la Nueva, a chapel and cloisters.

The Order of St John was created in 1113 by Pope Pascal II. It originated in Jerusalem and initially its members attended to the physical needs of the Christian pilgrims visiting that city. In order to fulfil these duties, the first Master of the Order, Gérard Tunc, ordered a church and a vast hospital, dedicated to St John the Baptist, to be built in Jerusalem. It was from this hospital that the Order took its name. Its members were divided into three groups: the clerics, the servants and attendants of the sick, and the knights. All of them had

221

taken the three vows of obedience, chastity and poverty; but the knights had in addition to fight the Infidels. It was inevitable, since the pilgrims required armed protection, that the emphasis on the Order's function should shift from the charitable to the military. The might of Islam, however, proved stronger than the Hospitalers and their brothers, the Templars. Eventually their possessions in the Holy

Consuegra

[8] Menéndez Pidal: *El Cid Campeador*, 1950.

Land fell one by one into the hands of their enemies and after the fall of their last bastion at St John of Acre in May, 1291, the Hospitalers were transferred to Cyprus. From there they moved to Rhodes in 1309. Their implacable enemies, the Turkish sultans, gave no respite to the Order of St John which had become a maritime power in the fourteenth century, in order to keep open the trade routes to the Holy Land. After massive attacks, Soliman the Magnificent conquered the almost impregnable citadel of Rhodes in 1522 after an epic siege lasting six months. It was Charles V who, understanding that the Order was in danger of disintegrating after this defeat, offered the Hospitalers the island of Malta, in a letter to Pope Clement VII, in 1528. From that time the Knights Hospitaler became known as the Knights of Malta.

The Order of St John took part in the Spanish Reconquest, and fought at Las Navas de Tolosa under the Prior of Castile, Gutierre de Armildez. The Order was particularly important in Aragón, where it built the famous castle-convent of Loarre; but its power extended also towards Castile. Consuegra was one of the castles of the Hospitalers in Castile and it was basically a place of physical and spiritual preparation or *noviciado* for the young men entering the Order.

The Order of St John of Jerusalem, later integrated into the Order of Malta, had for many years a feminine counterpart in Spain, the Lady Hospitalers of St John, who devoted themselves to hospital works and acts of charity. Beatrix Cornel, Prioress of the Convent of Sigena in Aragón was a member of this order. A fifteenth-century painting shows her on her deathbed with the emblem of the Order of St John, a black tunic with a white Maltese cross (the original version had a fork at the end of each arm, making eight points) of white linen on the left shoulder.

In the twelfth century Consuegra witnessed one of the worst defeats of Alfonso VI. The king, who had reconquered Toledo in 1085, was threatened by the invading armies of the Almorávides under the command of the powerful and cautious Yusef. He had said of his soldiers led by Mohammed Ben Ali: 'If God has decreed that they should be defeated, I, remaining behind them as a mantle, will cover their withdrawal.'[8] When Yusef pushed towards Toledo, Alfonso positioned himself in front of Consuegra. The Almorávides, organized in bodies of armed warriors, advanced in time to a drumbeat, presenting a formidable challenge. They carried the day, since according to the Arab chronicle 'the Almighty had sent confusion' into the Christian vanguard. It was August 15, 1097. The Cid's son was among the dead. Alfonso, defeated, took refuge in the castle of Consuegra and was besieged by the Arabs for eight days. Then, as suddenly as they had appeared, the Almoravid invaders withdrew.

CHRONOLOGY

c.1100 The port of Cádiz is founded by the Phoenicians. The Peninsula enters into a period of colonization by Mediterranean cultures: Phoenicians, Greeks, Carthaginians.

218 After the Punic Wars and the destruction of Carthage, Rome begins the conquest of Iberia.

133 The city of Numantia falls into Roman hands.

2 Seneca the Younger is born in Córdoba.

A.D.

61 Spain begins its conversion to Christianity.

117 Death of Trajan. Born near Seville, Trajan and later Hadrian are examples of the Spanish contribution to the Roman Empire.

414 The Visigoths cross the Pyrenees and spread quickly southwards meeting little opposition.

589 At Toledo, capital of his kingdom, the Visigothic king Reccared is converted to Catholicism.

711 **Arab invasion.** A Moorish army crosses from Africa to Gibraltar and destroys the Visigothic army of King Roderic at Guadalete.

718 The Arabs occupy most of the Iberian Peninsula except Galicia and the Asturias. King Pelayo manages to transform the battle of Covadonga into a victory. From the north-western extremities of Spain, the slow process of the Reconquest is put in motion.

731 The Arabs, having crossed the Pyrenees with great impetus, are finally stopped by Charles Martel at Tours.

929 Caliphate of Córdoba. Ruled by Abd-ar-Rahman III, the Arabs reach the highest point in the cultural and scientific development of Al-Andalus, as Moorish Spain was known.

997 The powerful Arab *caudillo* Al-Mansur raids the city of Santiago, but leaves untouched the shrine of the Apostle Saint James. The bells of the shrine, however, are brought back to Córdoba on the shoulders of the captives as a trophy and eventually melted into lamps for the city's great Mosque.

1002 Al-Mansur, master of the castle of Gormaz, suffers a serious defeat at Calatañazor.

1031 Abolition of the Caliphate.

1043 Birth of Ruy (or Rodrigo) Diaz de Vivar, the Cid (d.1099).

1085 King Alfonso VI enters Toledo, the first major Saracen city to be reconquered.

1086 Invasion of the Almorávides or Murabits.

1088 Raymond of Burgundy begins the reconstruc-
-90 tion of the walls of Avila.

1092 The Cid takes Valencia after a fifty-day siege.

1110 Invasion of the fanatic Almorávides (Arab holy warriors) who destroy San Servando.

1124 Sigüenza finally secured for the Christians by Bernardo de Agen.

1140 The Poem of the Cid: the first literary work to appear in the Castilian tongue.

1146 Invasion of the Almohades or Unitarians.

1195 Alfonso VIII of Castile defeated at Alarcos.

1212 Alfonso VIII destroys the Arab armies at the decisive battle of Las Navas de Tolosa.

1236 Ferdinand III wrests back Córdoba.

1248 Seville falls into the hands of Ferdinand III.

1254 Alfonso X, the Learned, obtains from Pope Alexander IV recognition, throughout Christendom, of the Degrees awarded by the University of Salamanca. Thus this University becomes one of the four major centres of learning in all Europe, together with Paris, Bologna and Oxford.

1333 Birth of Henry II, King of Castile and founder of the House of Trastamara.

1400 The castle of Coca, a unique example of *Mudéjar* design, is begun by Don Alonso de Fonseca, Archbishop of Seville.

1406 John II becomes king of Castile. His reign, lasting almost half a century, almost causes the collapse of the house of Trastamara, and is dominated by Don Alvaro de Luna, the royal favourite.

1425 Birth of Henry IV, the Impotent.

1451 Isabella, daughter of John II and Isabella of Portugal and half sister of Henry IV, is born at Madrigal de las Altas Torres.

1457 Work begins on the Castle-palace of Belmonte (Cuenca).

1462 Birth of Juana La Beltraneja, Isabella's rival for the Castilian crown. Historians are not agreed on the paternity of this unhappy pawn in the shameful manoeuvres for political power in the fifteenth century. Her contemporaries believed

Juana to be the daughter of Henry IV's favourite Don Beltrán de la Cueva, hence the nickname La Beltraneja.

1474 Isabella is crowned Queen of Castile in Segovia.

1478 The Inquisition is introduced in Castile.

1487 After three months of siege, the Arab stronghold of Málaga falls into the hands of Isabella's husband, Ferdinand of Aragón.

1492 This is called the *annus mirabilis* in Spanish history. On January 2, their Catholic majesties, Ferdinand and Isabella, receive the keys of the city of Granada from Boabdil, last Moorish ruler in Al-Andalus.

The Reconquest is over.

The Jews are expelled from Spain.
Columbus discovers America.

1504 Isabella dies at Medina del Campo.

1508 Cardinal Cisneros creates the University of Alcalá de Henares.

1520 Unsuccessful revolt of the Comuneros supporting Joanna the Mad, Isabella's daughter, against Charles V.

1540 Saint Ignacio de Loyola creates the Jesuit Order.

1547 Miguel de Cervantes is born at Alcalá de Henares.

1556 Charles V abdicates the Spanish Crown in favour of his son Philip II.

1561 Philip II chooses Madrid as the capital of Spain.

1571 Victory of Lepanto over the Turks.

1583 Construction of Villaviciosa de Odón.

1584 Juan de Herrera, architect of Philip II, completes the Escorial.

1588 The great Armada is destroyed by the English.

1598 Death of Philip II.

1605 First part of *Don Quixote* published by Cervantes.

1609 Expulsion of the Moriscos, as the Moors who lived as vassals of Christian kings were called.

1700 End of the house of Austria with the death of Charles II.

1710 Destruction of the Alcázar of Toledo during the War of the Spanish Succession. This was a civil war which began on the death of Charles II. Castile sided with Philip V of Bourbon, supported by France, while Catalonia favoured Archduke Charles of Austria, supported by England.

1713 End of the War of the Spanish Succession with the Treaty of Utrecht, whereby Spain loses all her European possessions.

1808 Napoleon invades Spain, beginning the bitter War of Independence that is to last until 1814.

1810 First signs of moves towards independence in Latin America.

1833 First Carlist War between supporters of Isabella II (Liberals) and Don Carlos (Conservatives), which lasted seven years.

1876 End of the third and last of the Carlist Wars.

1898 Independence of Cuba and Philippines following the war with the United States.

1923 Dictatorship of Primo de Rivera during the reign of Alfonso XIII.

1930 Fall of Alfonso XIII.

1931 Spain becomes a Republic.

1933 José Antonio Primo de Rivera creates the Falange.

1936 The Alcázar of Toledo is destroyed during the Civil War.

1939 The Civil War ends three days after the fall of Madrid on April 28.

THE RULERS OF CASTILE, AND LATER OF ALL SPAIN, FROM
ALFONSO VII TO JOSEPH BONAPARTE

Castile

1126–1157	Alfonso VII
1157–1158	Sancho III
1158–1188	Alfonso VIII
1188–1214	Alfonso IX
1214–1217	Henry I

León & Castile

1217–1252	Ferdinand III, the Saint
1252–1284	Alfonso X, the Wise
1284–1295	Sancho IV, the Brave
1295–1312	Ferdinand IV
1312–1350	Alfonso XI
1350–1369	Peter I, the Cruel
1369–1379	Henry II, of Trastamara
1379–1390	John I
1390–1406	Henry III, the Sickly
1406–1454	John II
1454–1474	Henry IV, the Impotent

Spain

1474–1504	Isabella I, of Castile, and Ferdinand II of Aragón (1479–1504)
1504–1506	Philip I, the Handsome, and Joanna the Mad
1506–1516	Ferdinand V (Ferdinand II, Regent, became in 1512 Ferdinand V, King of all Spain)
1516–1556	Charles I, of Spain (became Charles V, Holy Roman Emperor, elected 1519, crowned 1520)
1556–1598	Philip II
1598–1621	Philip III
1621–1665	Philip IV
1665–1700	Charles II
1700–1746	Philip V, Duke of Anjou. (Louis I reigned 1724 for a few months)
1746–1759	Ferdinand VI
1759–1788	Charles III
1788–1808	Charles IV
1808–1813	Joseph Bonaparte

BIBLIOGRAPHY

On castles:

Spanish sources

Bisso, José. CASTILLOS Y TRADICIONES FEUDALES DE LA PENINSULA IBERICA. Madrid, 1870.

Bordejé, Federico. CASTLES ITINERARY IN CASTILE. Madrid, 1965.

Colorado y Laca, Eugenio. EL CASTILLO DE TUREGANO; Estudios Segovianos. 1956.

Dotor, Angel. CASTILLOS DE SEGOVIA Y VALLADOLID.
CASTILLOS DE GUADALAJARA Y CUENCA.
CASTILLOS DE AVILA Y MADRID.
CASTILLOS DE TOLEDO. All published by the Revista Geográfica Española, Madrid.

Gamazo, Conde de. CASTILLOS EN CASTILLA. Madrid, 1955.

Lampérez y Romea, V. ARQUITECTURA CIVIL ESPAÑOLA (Vol. I). Madrid, 1922.
EL CASTILLO DE LA CALAHORRA; Boletin de la Sociedad Española de Excursiones. 1914.
EL CASTILLO DE BELMONTE; Boletin de la Sociedad Española de Excursiones. 1917.

Layna Serrano, Francisco. CASTILLOS DE GUADALAJARA. Madrid, 1933.

Navarro, Felipe B. FORTALEZAS Y CASTILLOS DE LA EDAD MEDIA (Maqueda y Escalona). Madrid, 1895.

Ortiz Echagüe, José. ESPAÑA: CASTILLOS Y ALCAZARES. Madrid, 1956.

Paz, J. CASTILLOS Y FORTALEZAS DEL REINO; Revista de Archivos, Bibliotecas y Museos. Madrid, 1895.

Quadrado, J. Ma. ESPAÑA: SUS MONUMENTOS Y ARTE. SU NATURALEZA E HISTORIA (CASTILLA LA NUEVA), Y VICENTE DE LA FUENTE. Barcelona, 1885.

Sainz de Robles, F. CASTILLOS EN ESPAÑA. Madrid, 1962.

Sarthou Carreres, Carlos. CASTILLOS DE ESPAÑA. Madrid, 1952.

Valenzuela Foved, Virgilio. EL CASTILLO DE LOARRE. Huesca, 1957.

ASOCIACION ESPAÑOLA DE AMIGOS DE LOS CASTILLOS: Articles by various authors.

Other sources: on Spanish castles

Bevan, Bernard. HISTORY OF SPANISH ARCHITECTURE. London, 1939.

Bodo, E. BURGENFAHRT DURCH SPANIEN. Marksburg, 1934.

Pillement, G. PALAIS ET CHATEAUX ARABES D'ANDALOUSIE. Paris, 1961.

Raggio, Olga. THE VELEZ BLANCO PATIO; Metropolitan Museum of Art Bulletin. December 1964.

Terrasse, H. LES FORTERESSES DE L'ESPAGNE MUSULMANE. Madrid, 1954.

Washburn, Oliver. CASTLES IN SPAIN. Mexico City, 1957.

On European castles

Clark, G. T. MEDIEVAL MILITARY ARCHITECTURE IN ENGLAND. London, 1884.

Cruden, Stewart. THE SCOTTISH CASTLE. 1963.

Deschamps, Paul. LES CHATEAUX DES CROISES EN TERRE-SAINTE. 1931.

Douglas Simpson, W. SCOTTISH CASTLES: AN INTRODUCTION TO THE CASTLES OF SCOTLAND. Edinburgh, 1959.
DOUNE CASTLE.
EXPLORING CASTLES. London, 1957.

Hohler, Christopher. KINGS AND CASTLES (Chapter: 'The Flowering of the Middle Ages'). London, 1966.

Jardot, Maurice. CHATEAUX DE LA LOIRE. Paris, 1952.

O'Neil, B. H. St. J. CASTLES: AN INTRODUCTION TO THE CASTLES OF ENGLAND AND WALES. London, 1954.

Taylor, A. J. CONWAY CASTLE AND TOWN WALLS. Ministry of Works Official Guide. London, 1961.

Toy, Sidney. A HISTORY OF FORTIFICATION from 3000 B.C. to A.D. 1700. London, 1955.
THE CASTLES OF GREAT BRITAIN. London, 1953.
Tuulse. CASTLES OF THE WESTERN WORLD. London, 1952.
GUIDE TO THE PARKS AND CHATEAUX OF FRANCE, La Demeure Historique. Foreword by the Duc de Luynes. Paris, 1960.

General Bibliography
Spanish publications
Lampérez y Romea, V. ARQUITECTURA CRISTIANA ESPAÑOLA. Madrid, 1906.
Lozoya, Juan de Contreras, Marqués de. HISTORIA DEL ARTE HISPANICO. Madrid, 1940.
Marañón, Gregorio. ENSAYO BIOLOGICO SOBRE ENRIQUE IV DE CASTILLA Y SU TIEMPO. Madrid, 1947.
Mariana, Juan de. HISTORIA GENERAL DE ESPAÑA. 1854.
Menéndez Pidal, Ramon. FLOR NUEVA DE ROMANCES VIEJOS. Buenos Aires, 1965.
EL CID CAMPEADOR. Madrid, 1950.
Ortega y Gasset, José CASTILLA. Madrid, 1942.
Quintana, M. J. VIDAS DE ESPAÑOLES CELEBRES: (EL PRINCIPE DE VIANA; EL GRAN CAPITAN). Madrid, 1966.
Salva, Jaime. LA ORDER DE MALTA. Madrid, 1944.
Unamuno, Miguel de. POR TIERRAS DE PORTUGAL Y ESPAÑA. Madrid, 1941.

French, English and German publications
Ali, Ameer. A SHORT HISTORY OF THE SARACENS. London, 1949.
Castro, Américo. THE STRUCTURE OF SPANISH HISTORY. Princeton, 1954.
Cirici-Pellicer, Alexandre. THE TREASURES OF SPAIN (FROM CHARLES V TO GOYA). Introduction by F. J. Sanchez Cantón. Geneva, 1965.
Cleator, P. E. CASTLES AND KINGS. London, 1960.
Creasy, Sir Edward S. FIFTEEN DECISIVE BATTLES OF THE WORLD. London, 1851.
Descola, Jean. HISTOIRE D'ESPAGNE. Paris, 1960.
Evans, Joan. ART IN MEDIEVAL FRANCE (987-1498). Oxford University Press, 1948.

Held, Robert. THE AGE OF FIREARMS. New York, 1957.
Hell, Vera and Helmut. THE GREAT PILGRIMAGES OF THE MIDDLE AGES. New York, 1966.
Herold, J. Christopher. THE AGE OF NAPOLEON. New York.
Hole, Edwyn. ANDALUS: SPAIN UNDER THE MUSLIMS. London, 1958.
Merriman, Roger Bigelow. THE RISE OF THE SPANISH EMPIRE (Vols. I & II). New York, 1918.
Merwin, W. S. THE POEM OF THE CID: A VERSE TRANSLATION. London, 1959.
Miller, Townsend. THE CASTLES AND THE CROWN. New York, 1963.
Nicolson, Harold. KINGS, COURTS AND MONARCHY. New York, 1962.
Pevsner, Nikolaus. AN OUTLINE OF EUROPEAN ARCHITECTURE; Pelican Books. London, 1963.
Pirenne, Henri. MOHAMMED AND CHARLEMAGNE. New York, 1939.
Pirenne, Jacques. THE TIDES OF HISTORY (Vol. II) New York, 1962.
Pratt, Fletcher. THE BATTLES THAT CHANGED THE WORLD. New York, 1956.
Prescott, William H. HISTORY OF THE REIGN OF FERDINAND AND ISABELLA. New York, 1837.
Treece, Henry. THE CRUSADES. New York, 1962.
Uhde, Bernard. BAUDENKMÄLER IN SPANIEN UND PORTUGAL. Berlin, 1892.

INDEX

Abasurto 205
Abd-ar-Rahman III 14, 16, 20, 214
Acuña, Don Antonio de, Bishop of Zamora 82
Agen, Bernardo de, Bishop 95
Aigues-Mortes (Provence) 55, 111, 168
Alarcón (Cuenca) 84
Alarcos, Battle of 21, 190, 210
Alba, House of 131
Alburquerque 39, 114, 116
Alcalá de Guadaira (Seville) 29, 178
Alcalá de Henares (Madrid) 55, 149, *163*
Alcántara, Bridge of *168*, 172
Alcántara, Order of 52, 190, 200, 204, 205
Alcázar of Madrid *149*
Alcázar of Segovia 40, 48, 124, 127, *142*, 149
Alcázar of Seville 128
Alcázar of Toledo 143, 149, 169, *186*
Alexander III, Pope 198, 204
Alexander VI, Pope 70
Alfonso, Infante (brother of Isabella) 120
Alfonso I, King of Aragón 190, 196
Alfonso I, King of León 86
Alfonso III, King of León 91
Alfonso VI (the Valiant), King of León & Asturias
    20, 21, 55, 88, 91, 111, 149, 166, 171, 172, 175,
    186, 214, 218, 223
Alfonso VII, King of León & Castile 20, 92, 172,
    196, 198, 209, 220
Alfonso VIII, King of Castile 21, 24, 69, 94, 142,
    190, 200, 204, 210, 212, 217
Alfonso X (the Learned), King of León & Castile
    60, 124, 142, 175, 186
Alfonso XI, King of León & Castile 60
Alhambra of Granada (or Calat Alhamra) 30
Aliama, Order of San Jorge de 205
Almansa (Murcia) 48
Al-Mansur (or Almanzor) 80, 84, 86, 88, 91, 149,
Arévalo (Avila) 51, 106, *118*, 120, 123, 128
Arragel, Rabbi 205, 220
Asalto, Count of 183, 184
Almodóvar del Rio (Córdoba) 30
Alvárez, Diego 175
Alvárez, Domingo 175
Anguix (Guadalajara) 13, 40, 47, 84, 198, 206, *217*
Anne of Austria (wife of Philip II) 143
Arenas de San Pedro (Avila) 106, *117*, 173
Arévalo (Avila) 50, 106, *119*, 123, 128

Asociación Española de Amigos de los Castillos 13,
    91, 173
Atienza (Guadalajara) 40, 47, 52, 55, 84, 90, *91*,
Aunqueospese (Avila) 106
Avila 51, 53, 55, *106*, 168, 216
Ayala, Pedro López de, 1st Count of Fuensalida
    183
Barciense (Toledo) 96, *173*
Beaumaris (Wales) 35, 100
Belalcázar 205
Bellver 35
Belmonte (Cuenca) 35, 84, *99*
Beltrán de la Cueva, Duke of Alburquerque 70,
    114, 116, 137, 138, 149
Benavente 198
Berenguer III, King of Barcelona 190
St. Bernard (Bernard de Clairvaux) 193
Blanca, Queen (wife of Peter I) 186, 220
Bordejé, Federico 61, 79, 111, 127, 142, 173
Borgia, Caesar 70, 72
Bothwell (Scotland) 113
Buitrago (Madrid) 18, 40, 55, 146, *150*
Cabrera, Don Diego Fernández de 164
Calahorra, La (Granada) 39, 45
Calatañazor, Battle of 88, 91
Calatrava La Nueva (Ciudad Real) 32, 40, 45, 47,
    55, 198, 200, 206, *110*, *211*, 221
Calatrava La Vieja (Ciudad Real) 18, 29, 47, 178,
    198, *209*, 212
Calatrava, Order of 23, 45, 47, 61, 82, 84, 92, 173,
    190, 194, 198, 200, 205, 210, 211, 212, 214, 216,
    218, 220
Caliphate of Córdoba 20, 26, 56, 88
Carcassonne 55, 168
Cárdenas, Diego de 220
Carlos, Don 96
Carmona 29
Carreño, Fernando de 69, 70
Carreres, Sarthou 13, 84
Carrillo, Don Alonso, Archbishop of Toledo 45, 97,
    111, 127, 149
Cassandro 108
Castel del Monte (Italy) 35, 100
Castelnuovo (or Maschio Angioino) 52, 72
Castilnovo (Segovia) 70, 124, *140*
Castro, Américo 193, 194
Cervantes, Miguel de 149
Charlemagne 203
Charles, Archduke of Austria 96
Charles V, Emperor (Charles I of Spain) 56, 76,
    80, 123, 149, 166, 168, 186, 206, 223
Charles III, King of Spain 127, 186
Charles IV, King of Spain 164
Charles Martel 14,
Chastel Blanc (Palestine) 127

Chinchón (Madrid)   146, *162*
Christian III, King of Denmark & Sweden   54
El Cid, Rodrigo (Ruy) Díaz de Vivar   84, 88, 90,
    91, 95, 171, 172, 186, 214
Ciruelos   198, 210
Cisneros, Cardinal   80, 95, 149, 164
Clairvaux, Bernard de, *see* St. Bernard
Clement V, Pope   194
Clement VII, Pope   223
Coca (Segovia)   35, 39, 124, 126,
    128, 150, 172, 219
Colchester (Essex)   51
Colmenares   135
Colorado y Laca, Eugenio   127
Columbus, Christopher   25, 142
Consuegra (Toledo)   40, 168, 172, *221*
Conway (Wales)   37, 44, 55, 63, 64, 111
Cornel, Beatrix   223
Coucy   40
Covadonga, Battle of   17, 25
Covarrubias   186
Craigmillar (Scotland)   135
Crest (Drôme)   51
Cruden, S. H.   33
Cuéllar (Segovia)   124, 128, *137*
Dávalos, Don Ruy López   117
Dávila, Don Pedro, Marquis of Las Navas   123
Dávila, Juan Arias, Bishop of Segovia   126, 127
Dotor, Don Angel, 200, 204
Douglas, Sir James   42
Doune (Scotland)   35, 120
Eboli, Princess of   149
Echagüe, Ortiz   131
Edward I, King of England   34, 113
Edward, the Black Prince   42, 44
Escalona (Toledo)   40, 42, 44, 168, *175*, 220
Escorial   123, 157, 186
Eugene III, Pope   193
Eugenia, Empress (wife of Napoleon III)   105
Fañez, Alvar   214
Fatho-ben-Ibrahim   218
Ferdinand I (the Great), King of Castile   95
Ferdinand II of Aragón   24, 25, 45, 53, 69, 76, 87,
    119, 127, 138, 140, 154, 206, 212
Ferdinand II, King of León   94
Ferdinand III (the Saint), King of León & Castile
    24, 29, 142
Ferdinand VI (the Wise), King of Spain   164
Ferdinand VII, King of Spain   164
Fernández de Córdoba, Don Gonzalo   52, 72
Fitero, Fray Raimundo de   198, 210
Flint (Wales)   113
Fonseca, Alfonso de, Archbishop of Seville   45, 128,
    133
Francis I, King of France   135

Francis, Duke of Angoulême   135
Frederick II, Holy Roman Emperor   35
Frias, Duke of   87, 134
Fuensaldaña (Valladolid)   35, 40, 45, 50, 56, 65,
    74, 75, 76, 80, 131
Gaillard, Château   32, 40
Galib   88
Gamazo, Count of   79, 82, 128
García, Sancho   60, 86, 88
García-Fernández   88
Garcimuñoz (Cuenca)   84, 99
Gibralfaro (Málaga)   29
Girón, Don Pedro   61, 205
Gisselfeld (Denmark)   120
Godoy, Manuel, Prince of La Paz   164, 165
González, Fernán, Count of Castile   59, 124
Gormaz (Soria)   18, 29, 84, 87, *88*, 209
Goyena, Duke of   70
Grajal de Campos (León)   54
Las Guadalerzas   *173*
Guadamur (Toledo)   140, 168, *183*
Guadalete, Battle of   166
Guas, Juan de   154
Gutierre de Armildez   223
Gutierre de Cárdenas   219
Guzmán, Fernán Gómez de   205
Guzmán, Don Luis de, Grand Master of Calatrava
    205
Hapsburg, House of   54, 76, 186
Haro (Cuenca)   *99*
Henry II, King of France   135
Henry II of Castile (Henry of Trastamara)   44, 150
Henry III (the Sickly), King of León & Castile   149
Henry IV (the Impotent), King of León & Castile
    39, 70, 94, 99, 102, 114, 117, 120, 124, 126, 128,
    137, 142, 149, 159, *176*, 205
Henry VIII, King of England   54
Herold, J. Christopher   164
Herrera, Juan de   80, 123, 143, 164, 165, 186,
Hospitallers   45, 47, 190, 193, 194, 196, 205, 221,
    222, 223
Hugo, Marshall   98
Ibn-Yusef   198, 210
Innocent III, Pope   21
Isabella of Castile (Isabella I of Spain)   13, 24, 25,
    45, 52, 56, 69, 70, 72, 76, 87, 94, 106, 116, 119,
    120, 127, 128, 137, 140, 142, 154, 159, 205, 206,
    212
Italicus, Silvo   86
Jaén, Battle of   172
Jaime the Conqueror   45
Jiménez de Rada, Rodrigo, Archbishop of Toledo
    190, 200
Joanna la Beltraneja (daughter of Henry IV)   70,
    102, 115, 137, 153, 159

Joanna the Mad (wife of Philip the Handsome)   56, 70, 76, 184

Joanna of Portugal (2nd wife of Henry IV)   116, 137, 149, 153

St. John of the Cross   105, 106

John I, King of León & Castile   142

John II, King of León & Castile   39, 45, 69, 76, 82, 93, 124, 128, 140, 142, 153, 154, 161, 175, 205

Juan of Austria, Don   146, 162

Krak des Chevaliers   196

Lampérez y Romea, Vicente   44, 66, 102, 108, 126, 154, 173, 178

Leo XIII, Pope   174

León, Fray Luis de   105

Leovigild, King   214

Lepanto, Battle of   146, 162

Livy   94

Loarre (Huesca)   47, 223

López de Madrid, Don Diego   94, 95

Louis VII, King of France   193

Louis XI, King of France   70

Luna, Don Alvaro de, Master of Calatrava & Constable of Castile   45, 76, 82, 93, 94, 117, 124, 140, 161, 175, 176, 178

Luna, Juana de   117

Malmöhus (Sweden)   54

Manrique, Jorge   99

Manuel, Infante Don Juan   60, 66, 67, 175

Maqueda (Toledo)   168, 175, 198, 206, *218*

Marañon, Gregorio   116

Maria Luisa (wife of Charles IV)   164

Marcellus   94

Martin, Juan   96, 98

Medinaceli, Duke of   84, 90, 106

Mendoza, Don Pedro González, Cardinal 94, 95, 96

Mendoza, Iñigo López de, Marquis of Santillana   97, 153, 154

Metellus   94, 95

Miller, Townsend   205

Mohammed-ben-Alhamar   30

Mohammed-ben-Ali   223

Mohammed al Nazir   21

Molai, Jacques de   194

Mombeltrán (Avila)   106, 111, *113*, 117

Montalbán (Toledo)   153, 168

Montealegre (Valladolid)   48, 153

Montesa, Order of   205

Montoya, Bishop   87

Mora, Francisco de   143

Moscardó, General   186

La Mota, Medina del Campo (Segovia)   32, 34, 40, 56, 66, *67*, 69, 70, 72, 74

Nájera, Battle of   44

Napoleon   165

Narbonne   14, 17

Navarro, Felipe   219

Las Navas de Tolosa, Battle of   21, 23, 24, 173, 190, 200, 210, 217, 223

Las Navas del Marqués, or Magalia, (Avila)   53, 54, 106, *123*, 163, 165, 186

Nebrija, Antonio de   205

Nieto, Alonso   69

Numantia, Siege of   26, 86, 94, 95

Nuñez de Prado, Don Juan   220

Obeidala   218

Olmedo   55, 118, 128

Ordoñez, Martin   217

Ortega y Gasset, José   13, 91

Osma (Soria)   59, *86*

Pacheco, Don Juan, Marquis of Villena   84, 87, 99, 102, 124, 176, 205

Padilla, Don Juan de   56

Padilla, Doña María   186

Palencia   116

Pascal II, Pope   190, 221

Pastrana, Duke of   149, 174, 216

Pavia, Battle of   135

Paynes, Hugh de   193

Pedraza (Segovia)   47, 55, 124, *133*,

Pelayo, King   17, 124

Peñafiel (Valladolid)   17, 32, 35, 39, 44, 48, 51, 56, *58*, 79, 88, 131

Peñiscola   205

Pepin of Heristal   14

Pereiro, San Julian del (Portuguese Order)   204

Pérez, Antonio   127

Peter I (the Cruel), King of León & Castile   44, 76, 128, 150, 186, 220

Peter II of Aragón   190

Pevsner, Nicholas   100

Philip I of Spain (the Handsome)   184, 194

Philip II, King of Spain   80, 82, 96, 123, 127, 143, 146, 149, 157, 164, 186, 212, 216

Philip V (Duke of Anjou), first Bourbon King of Spain   48, 150, 164, 218

Pimentel, Juana de   117, 176

Pioz (Guadalajara)   96

Pius V, Pope   149

Pizarro, Hernando   72

Pliny   86

Ponferrada (León)   47, 196

Ponthieux, Florián de   108

Pompey   86, 94, 95

Puelles, Juan de   97

Quintana, M. J.   52, 70, 175

Quintanar, Marquis of   140

Racupel   30

Ramiro II, King of León   149

Rasis (Moslem Chronicler)   214

Ravenscraig (Fife)   53, 54

Raymond of Burgundy   55, 108, 111
Real de Manzanares (Madrid)   39, 95, 146, *154*, 198
Reccared, King of Visigothic Spain   14, 166, 214
Requesens, Don Luis de   146, 162
Richard I (Coeur-de-Lion), King of England   32
Robert the Bruce, King of Scots   42
Rocroi, Battle of   23
Roderic (Visigothic King)   14
Rodriguez, Ventura   186
Rosminthal, Baron   124
Sacro Lirio, Baron of   159
Sagrajas, Battle of   172
Sainz de Robles, Federico   209
Salinas   105
Salses (Rousillon)   52
Salvatierra (Ciudad Real)   198, 200, 210, 212
Sancho III, King of Castile   198, 209
Sancho IV (The Brave), King of León and Castile   60
Sancho V, King of Navarre   24, 190
San Martín, Bridge of   *168*,
San Martín de Valdeiglesias   140, 146, *159*, 165
San Quintin, Battle of   157
San Servando (Toledo)   168, 169, *171*, 220
Santa Maria de Paso   150
Santa Maria del Campo   99
Santiago de Compostela   88, 196, 202, 203
Santiago, Order of   23, 84, 99, 176, 178, 190, 200, 202, 204
Scipio   94
Segontia, *see* Sigüenza
Sepúlveda (Segovia)   124, 140
Serrano, Layna   92, 95, 214
Sigüenza (Guadalajara)   84, *94*, 126, 172
Simancas (Valladolid)   74, *80*, 143
Soliman the Magnificent   223
Sotomayor, Francisco de   52
Stahrenberg, General   164, 186
Stirling (Scotland)   34
Suchet, General   178
Tarifa   14
Tarik the One-Eyed   14
Téllez, Gonzalo   86
Templars   45, 47, 48, 96, 127, 168, 172, 190, 193, 194, 196, 209, 222
Tenorio, Pedro (Archbishop of Toledo)   164, 172, 220
St. Teresa of Avila   106
Tordesillas (Valladolid)   56, 66, 76, 80
Torija (Guadalajara)   13, 40, 52, *96*, 123
Tormo, Don Elías   128
Toro, Battle of   94, 154
Torre del Clavero (Salamanca)   52
Torrelobatón (Valladolid)   39, 40, 48, 50, 51, 67

La Torrona   51
Tours, Battle of   14, 16
Tower of London   51
Trajan, Emperor   135
Trastamara, House of   32
Troyes, Council of   193
Tunc, Gérard   221
Turégano (Segovia)   124, *126*, 172
Tuulse   75
Uceda, Duke of   87
Ucera   87
Uclés   20, *84*, 99, 172
Ulaca   111
Unamuno, Miguel de   106
Valcárcel, J. M. Gonzalez   96
Valde-Corneja   106
Vázquez, Diego   198, 210
Vázquez, Lorenzo   39
Vega, Lope de   205
Vela, Torre de (Toledo)   219, 220
Velazco, Torrejón de   146
Velez Blanco, Marquis of   157
Vendôme, Duke of   164
Vienne, Council of   194
Villafuerte   50
Villalain   96
Villalar, Battle of   82
Villalonso   40, 50
Villapando   186
Villarejo de Salvanés (Madrid)   52, 146, *161*
Villaviciosa (Avila)   *111*
Villaviciosa de Odón (Madrid)   163, *164*
Villena, Marquises of   84, 87, 99, 102, 124, 176, 205
Vincennes, Château de   40, 75
Visby (Sweden)   55, 111, 168
Vivar, Rodrigo Díaz de, *see* El Cid
Vivero, Don Alfonso Perez de   76
Vivero, Don Juan de, Count of Fuensaldaña   76
Wadhah   218
Walled City of Avila   *106*
War of the Comuneros   56, 76, 138, 164
War of the Comunidades   50, 142
War of the Spanish Succession   13, 96, 138, 163, 186, 218
Wellington, Duke of   138
Los Yebenes (Toledo)   173
Yusef-ibn-Tashfin   20, 223
Zacuto, Abraham   205
Zalamea   205
Zorita de los Canes (Guadalajara)   40, 47, 84, 92, 198, 200, 206, 210, *212*, 214, 218
Zorrilla, Juan   80
Zuloaga   135
Zuñiga, Don Alvaro de, Count of Plasencia   120
Zuñiga, Don Juan de   205